'Alister McGrath has written an intellectual thriller that documents his transition from a nature-loving schoolboy Marxist to the Oxford Professor of Science and Religion. The detail is fascinating: discovering that what once was certain crumbled, probing the methods and limits of science and finding in literature, historical, philosophical and imaginative, a pathway from the shadows of Plato's cave to an epiphany of understanding in the sunlit uplands, similar to that of C.S. Lewis before him. Realising not only that science and religion give different but complementary maps of the world, but also that Christianity offers the coherent big-picture framework for which his mind and heart had been questing. This is a must read for all those interested in the life of the mind and the science–religion debate. I could not put it down. You will not be able to either.'

John Lennox, Emeritus Professor of Mathematics,
University of Oxford

'A compelling story, at once readable and profound. In charting his path from atheism to Christian faith, Alister McGrath offers rich resources for believers, as well as a robust challenge to sceptics and religion's cultured despisers.'

Rupert Shortt, author of *Outgrowing Dawkins: God for Grown-Ups*

'Alister McGrath is renowned as a world-leading academic and very successful author with a particular interest in the interface of science and religion. This readable account tells his personal story and might even become a classic. It portrays his journey from a young prodigy to scientist and theologian. Enlivened with occasional flashes of humour and drawing on the author's exceptional breadth and depth of reading, it illustrates why he has successfully written for popular as well as academic audiences. It deserves to be very widely read.'

Michael J. Reiss, President, International Society for Science and Religion

'A personal story of how Alister McGrath travelled from a youthful certainty of atheism, across troubled intellectual seas, to arrive on an island of faith where he learned to be at peace with uncertainty . . . McGrath explains why Christianity, in providing the big picture which accommodates science, is not only plausible but intellectually satisfying. *Through a Glass Darkly* is a book that will help anyone wishing, with sincerity and intellectual honesty, to reconsider the apparent conflict between science and Christian faith. They will find, as did McGrath, that "understanding what is going on" does not demand total certainty, that living with uncertainty is not an admission of failure but a recognition of reality and that faith in God is the way to peace.'

Paul Ewart, Professor of Physics, University of Oxford

Through a Glass Darkly

Journeys through Science, Faith and Doubt
– a Memoir

Alister McGrath

HODDER

First published in Great Britain in 2020 by Hodder & Stoughton
An Hachette UK company

This paperback edition first published 2021

1

A CIP catalogue record for this title is available from the British Library

Paperback ISBN 978 1 529 32762 5
eBook ISBN 978 1 529 32763 2

Typeset in Sabon MT by Hewer Text UK Ltd, Edinburgh
Printed and bound in Great Britain by Clays Ltd, Elcograf S.p.A.

Hodder & Stoughton policy is to use papers that are natural, renewable
and recyclable products and made from wood grown in sustainable
forests. The logging and manufacturing processes are expected to
conform to the environmental regulations of the country of origin.

Hodder & Stoughton Ltd
Carmelite House
50 Victoria Embankment
London EC4Y 0DZ

www.hodderfaith.com

Contents

Preface vii

Part One A Restless Freethinker:
     Discovering a New World

1 A Curious Mind 3

2 Science as Sense-Making 12

3 A Sceptical Chemist 22

4 Dreaming of Oxford 31

5 A Crisis of Faith 39

6 Discovering God 49

Part Two An Unexpected Conversion:
     Exploring a Strange New World

7 Shipwrecked on an Island of Faith 59

8 A Travelling Companion: C.S. Lewis 68

9 The First Mountain: Science 78

10 The Second Mountain: Theology 89

11 Wandering: Searching for a Calling 102

12 Oxford: Finding a Calling 113

13 The Two Peaks: The View from the Top 124

Part Three   Old Questions, New Insights:
             Living on the Island of Faith

14 On Reconsidering What Once Seemed Obvious   137

15 Seeing Reality: Christianity as a 'Big Picture'   141

16 Revisiting Plato's Cave: On Darkness, Shadows
    and Light   151

17 Longing for Certainty: Proof, Faith and Doubt   158

18 Delusion: Faith as Wish-Fulfilment?   169

19 Maps of Reality: Coping with the Complexity
    of Our World   176

20 Science and Faith: Conflicting or Enriching?   184

21 The Irrationality of Faith? The Doctrine of
    the Trinity   193

22 Through a Glass Darkly: Journeying through
    Doubt   202

23 A Loose Ending   209

    Some Notes on My Books   211

    Notes   215

Preface

This book tells the story of how I, a restless freethinking atheist with a love of science, found my way to an unfashionable but deeply rewarding, rational and resilient way of understanding the world that I discovered was called Christianity. It is not an autobiography, although biographical details are inevitably woven into my narrative of discovery and reflection. Nor is it a work of theology, although I touch on many theological issues. It is a story of the loss of my intellectual innocence in the face of a world that obstinately refused to conform to my preconceptions of what it ought to be like.

This short work is fundamentally an exploration of ideas, an account of intellectual journeys of discovery, in which I reflect on my growing awareness of the complexity of reality, the limits placed on our understanding of it, and their implications for my doomed youthful quest for a simple take on a complicated world. It involves my own shift from atheism to Christianity, set in the context of the cultural restlessness of the late 1960s, and my discovery of the exhilarating and rewarding discipline of theology while researching at Oxford University's Department of Biochemistry. For those who know me best through my theology textbooks, this book explains how those came to be written.

Although my transition from atheism to Christianity is an important component of this story, it is not the only journey of discovery I made over the course of my life. Alongside this change in my religious views, I learned that an early expectation of certainty in relation to the big questions of life was unsustainable. All of us, whether atheists or religious believers, have to learn to live with uncertainty about those beliefs that we think *really* matter – such as the existence of God, the nature of the good, or the meaning of life. I had to learn to live in a world in which we cannot prove our core convictions. The images of darkness and shadows loom large in this narrative, precisely because it explores how we can live meaningfully and authentically in the midst of uncertainty and doubt. It can be done.

Alister McGrath
Oxford, February 2020

PART ONE

A Restless Freethinker: Discovering a New World

I

A Curious Mind

I was ten years old. Captivated by the sheer beauty and vastness of the star-studded sky on cold and frosty Irish winter
nights, I had built myself a little telescope to allow me to see
it in greater detail. I pointed it towards the skies for the first
time and peered through the eyepiece. Time seemed to stand
still as the star-fields of the Milky Way suddenly came into
focus; I was overwhelmed by what I could see. It seemed to
me, if only for a moment, as though I were poised on the
brink of something – like standing on a beach, catching a
glimpse of the far distance. This was the moment I realised
that I wanted to be a scientist, looking at and understanding
the immensity of the world.

I wasn't on my own here. Since the beginning of history
people have been enthralled by the solemn stillness of the
star-filled night sky, wondering what it meant. The
ancient Greeks saw meaningful patterns in the stars, and
named these constellations after their heroes, such as
Orion the great hunter and Andromeda the doomed heroine. Others found that those bright jewels of light in the
midst of the cosmic blackness evoked an unspeakable
sense of longing for something that was as indefinable as
it was unattainable.

As a child I knew that feeling as I gazed entranced and
uncomprehendingly at the cold and beautiful brilliance of
the stars. Looking through my telescope made me restless to
explore, a restlessness increased by the seeming difficulty of

uncovering the mysteries of the night sky. I was probably only eleven or twelve years old when I resolved to set out on an adventure to discover as much as I could about the universe. I had no idea where this might take me, but I had a deep sense it would be rewarding and satisfying.

So who am I? I was born in the city of Belfast into a medical family in January 1953, the year of the coronation of Queen Elizabeth II. My father had been a junior doctor and my mother a nurse at the city's Royal Victoria Hospital. My mother was born in Lismore, a small Irish town in County Waterford. Its main landmark, Lismore Castle, stands on a steep hill, dominating both the town and the Blackwater valley below it. My grandfather had served in the British Army during the First World War, and had returned to Ireland after being wounded in combat. He married the nurse who tended him at a military dressing station near Dublin, and settled in Lismore. One of my clearest childhood memories is a large and rather beautiful oil painting of Lismore Castle, which hung in my grandparents' drawing room in Belfast. I had always assumed this was a memento of their early life together; much later, I learned there was more to it than that.

My mother's family was Protestant and found themselves caught up in the lingering sectarian conflict in Waterford arising from the aftermath of the Irish Civil War of the 1920s. They were given the option of voluntarily leaving their house in Lismore or being burned out. Finding themselves refugees from another of Europe's now long-forgotten conflicts, they initially found shelter in Dublin, before finally relocating to the mainly Protestant north of Ireland, where they would be safe. I only learned the story of what happened in Lismore from my mother ten years before her death, when

4

she and her brother decided to return and pay a last visit to the Eden from which they had been expelled.

By the time of my birth, my parents had moved to Downpatrick, the ancient and historic county town of County Down, where my father served as the county's Medical Officer of Health. I was baptised in Down Cathedral, the town's best-known landmark, famous as the traditional burial place of Patrick, patron saint of Ireland. One of my fondest childhood memories was sitting on a bench in the Cathedral's grounds on late summer afternoons, looking to the south towards the purple-headed Mountains of Mourne across the lush green patchwork of undulating fields and meadows that C.S. Lewis so aptly called the 'soft low hills of Down'.

I attended Down High School in Downpatrick, a short walk from the Cathedral. I seemed to have some natural aptitude for reading and mathematics, and found myself excelling at both without the inconvenience of having to work at them. The school's motto was *Floreat Dunum – Absque Labore Nihil* ('May Down flourish! Nothing without effort!'). I conveniently ignored the second element of this motto, which was so clearly contradicted by my own experience.

It didn't take me long to work out that I was both clever and lazy, so could get away with the minimum of effort and virtually no homework. I was much happier playing with friends, exploring the 'Mound of Down' (a megalithic hill-fort close to the school), or racing on my bicycle along nearby country lanes. Without really trying, I kept on winning school prizes in English and mathematics. Yet nature seems to balance things out. While I was good at some things, I was useless at others. For a start, I lacked physical coordination, and came to accept that I would never be any good at sport, art or playing music. My only real talent lay in the life of the mind.

When I was ten, our English literature teacher realised that he was going to finish his year's teaching two weeks early. Rather than allow us to do our homework during his lessons, he told us that he was going to read aloud to us a book he thought we might like – *Farmer Giles of Ham*. None of us had ever heard of it. (Twenty years later, I became aware that this was an early work of J.R.R. Tolkien.) Mr Archer made himself comfortable on his desk, cleared his throat, and began to read. I – and, I afterwards discovered, most of those present – were entranced by the narrative. I discovered for the first time how my imagination could be taken captive, leading me as a willing prisoner into a world of which I knew nothing – save that I wanted to be part of it, and explore it. Archer ran out of time, so we never discovered how the book ended.

On returning home after that final lesson, I began to explore the family bookshelves. There was no sign of *Farmer Giles of Ham*, but there were other titles that sounded promising, including *The Coral Island*, *Treasure Island* and *Robinson Crusoe*. Having devoured them, I looked for more, and stumbled across the detective novels of Agatha Christie, Dorothy L. Sayers and Margery Allingham. I had no idea that these three writers were leading representatives of the 'Golden Age' of British crime fiction during the 1930s; I simply fell in love with the genre, and went on to explore others – most notably, the Sherlock Holmes stories.

Detective fiction allowed me to indulge my emerging love of stories alongside my intuitive desire to try and make sense of things. I was invited to step into the fictional narrative, identifying the clues, and struggling to find their explanation. It was not irrational, yet it was somehow more than rational – almost like the construction of an imaginative vision of what had happened, discerning what lay beneath the surface of the narrative. When you grasped this deeper understanding, the original narrative was seen in a new way. I learned how to make sense of clues which in themselves proved nothing and pointed to many possibilities, but which *cumulatively* disclosed a wider picture – a single solution, a golden thread that held all the clues together in a deeply satisfying conclusion. I was hooked and began to read such novels and stories voraciously, relishing the different approaches to the genre I discovered.

My eyes were opened in another way about the same time too. I was becoming aware of the beauty and mystery of the natural world around me. During the early 1960s, we spent our annual family holiday in County Donegal, in the north-west of Ireland. I happily explored the shoreline and little pools of saltwater, clutching my copy of *The Seashore for Boys and Girls* (1954) to help me make sense of what I found. On good days we walked along the sands, taking in the salty smell of sea and seaweed, and watching the advancing lines of waves breaking gently on the beaches of the Silver Strand. (On bad days, we waited inside our car for the rain to stop, drinking endless cups of tea from a large Thermos flask as the windows misted up with condensing steam.)

The country lanes and rivers of County Down provided what Wordsworth so aptly described as 'fair seed-time' for my soul, prompting me to love nature and long to know more about it. Our family home in Downpatrick was only a few minutes' walk from the Quoile Pondage. My schoolfriends and I often played along the banks of the Quoile, seeing who could skim stones the farthest along its surface. Yet as I stooped down on the river's edge one day to find a suitable pebble, I found my attention being diverted to what was in the water – to the silky green filaments of algae growing on stones beneath the surface. A few days later, I went down to the river's edge on my own, and collected a small glass jar of water, trying to work out what was in it with a magnifying glass that my father used to peruse his collection of postage stamps of the British Commonwealth.

Shortly afterwards, a great-uncle who had retired as a pathologist at the Royal Victoria Hospital in Belfast gave me his old brass microscope, which he had bought while he was a medical student in the early 1900s. It was made by Ernst Leitz, a German specialist manufacturer of optical instruments that later achieved fame for its Leica cameras.[1] It worked perfectly for my purposes, opening up a new living world invisible to the naked eye.

What fascinated me most, though, was the night sky. When walking home from school events on cold winter's nights, I was often overwhelmed by the beauty of the starlit heavens above me. I learned the names of the constellations and the brighter stars, and began to read books on astronomy. It seemed so much more interesting than the rather dull science I was being taught at school.

Encouraged by my success with my great-uncle's microscope, I made a small telescope out of some old camera lenses, and was astonished at the rich vistas even this crude instrument made possible. My parents bought me a proper telescope shortly afterwards, allowing me to observe the moons of Jupiter, the mountains of the moon, and the faint fuzzy patches of light that I later learned were galaxies far beyond our own. I soon realised the limits placed on my own unaided vision. I saw darkly; the telescope enabled me to see more clearly. The night sky was far richer and more beautiful than I had ever thought possible. It was like discovering a new world, one that had always been present, but that I had until this point lacked the necessary clarity of vision to see.

Yet I was becoming conscious of a massive disparity between my growing technical and factual knowledge of astronomy and the sense of wonder or awe that I experienced in beholding the solemn stillness of the starlit canopy above me. I mentioned this to one of my English teachers at school. 'That's why we need poetry!', he declared, adding that science wasn't any good at dealing with feelings or beauty. He did not persuade me that science was *wrong*; he did, however, make me open to the possibility that it was *incomplete*, failing to address something important, deep and significant within human nature.

I knew – or at least *thought* I knew – what he was getting at. It was astonishing that such a complex universe existed; yet it seemed equally astonishing – and very special – that I was here to observe it, to experience such a sense of wonder at its beauty and intricacy, and to think about what it all meant. But how could I weave such a strongly subjective, even emotional, response to nature into the detached and objective accounts of science that I was learning to value? In the end, I set such thoughts to one side. Perhaps they were a distraction, getting in the way of more important things.

The teaching staff at Down High School certainly thought so, and began to express concern that I was not focusing enough on my coursework. My performance in school examinations was not what it had been in the past. It was obvious to the school that I was too easily distracted and was not putting in the hours of dedicated study at home that would ensure a strong examination performance, and hence a place at university. My parents agreed with this judgement, while feeling it was only part of the picture. They began to suspect – rightly – that I was intellectually understimulated. My explorations in astronomy were not a symptom of an inability to concentrate on my coursework, but rather an indication of a desire to go into things more deeply than the limited resources available at Down High School allowed. It was a fine educational establishment, but could not offer the specialist teaching in the natural sciences that I craved. I needed a big change.

In the end, it was my mother who worked out a solution. She had been educated at the Methodist College, Belfast – a grammar school known to my mother and just about everyone else as 'Methody'. The school – one of Ireland's largest – had a strong reputation in teaching the natural sciences. It accepted a small number of students as boarders, living on the school premises during term, although they were free to go home at weekends. Ernest Walton, Ireland's only Nobel Laureate at that time, had studied science at Methody as a boarder from 1915 to 1922, and gone on to share the Nobel Prize for Physics in 1951 for splitting the atom. In 1961 Stanley Worrall was appointed Headmaster, and presided over a significant expansion of the school's teaching facilities in the natural sciences. Methody was the obvious choice for someone like me who loved the sciences. It would allow me to specialise in chemistry, physics and biology as individual subjects.

My mother's solution, however, had two components: the first was designed to appeal to my love of science; the second was designed to break my crystallising habits of academic idleness before they overwhelmed me. Rather than travelling by bus daily between Downpatrick and south Belfast, I would be a boarder at Methody – and thus be required to do two hours supervised study every weekday evening during school term. This, my mother firmly believed, would help me overcome my complete lack of intellectual discipline.

My father was very happy with this possibility. Methody was across the street from Queen's University Belfast, where he had studied medicine in the 1940s. It would, he remarked, make my own move to Queen's much easier when the time came. Happily, however, I also had a say in this decision. I visited the school with my parents and was shown around its dormitories and science laboratories. As I walked around, meeting students and exploring the school's buildings, I had a curious sense of standing on a threshold, having to make a decision that would shape the rest of my life. What my mother was proposing would give me more independence, force me to work harder, and allow me to immerse myself in the academic fields I had come to love. I struggled to find a downside.

'So what do you think?', my mother asked me as we drove home afterwards. I cannot remember quite how I answered her, but I know it was to this effect: 'I think it will be good for me.' It was.

2

Science as Sense-Making

In September 1966, aged thirteen, I became a boarder at the Methodist College, Belfast, and settled into a new way of life. At that time, students at my stage spent two years studying a broad range of subjects at Ordinary Level, before moving into the sixth form to study a more restricted group of subjects at Advanced Level. Everyone was required to study English language, English literature, French and mathematics at O Level. Returning students at Methody had already decided what additional subjects they would take. As a new student, I had to make those decisions on the morning of my first day at school, so that my interests could be accommodated within the complex teaching timetable. I had a fifteen-minute meeting with my Form Master on my first day at school, who quizzed me about what I liked and what I thought I was good at. At the end of our discussion, he directed me to study additional mathematics, chemistry, physics and biology, and worked out my personal timetable with me.

The boarding department at Methody imposed two requirements on its students. First, they would attend church on Sundays; second, they would spend every weekday evening following through what had been learned in class that day, and doing any required reading or writing projects. Church attendance seemed to me both tedious and pointless, although I could understand its role, given Methody's history. Every Sunday, those of us who self-defined as being

'Church of Ireland' would walk up the Lisburn Road to St Thomas' Church for its service of Morning Prayer. I passed my time idly flicking through the Prayer Book, wondering what anyone could possibly find interesting about its verbally obscure and intellectually impenetrable Creeds.

I initially resented having to spend two hours every evening working on textbooks, but quickly came to appreciate the merits of this regime. As my mother had suspected, enforced study cured my habits of idleness. To my own surprise, I found I was not merely coping with the academic work but was actually enjoying it, especially in exploring the abstract structures of pure mathematics. As far as I could see, there was no practical benefit to knowing that the square root of two was an irrational number; yet I could not fail to be impressed with the elegance of the mathematical proof of this fact.

To my parents' surprise and alarm, I brought some school books home with me for the Christmas vacation, so that I could get ahead of my studies in preparation for the next term. I still read novels, of course, ransacking both my parents' bookcases and the school library to find new material to explore, and dabbled in some popular philosophy – Pascal being a favourite, mainly because he could be brief and pithy, but partly because he was such a significant pure mathematician. Reading novels, however, was now a supplement to my studies, rather than an alternative to them. I found a deep satisfaction in the pursuit of ideas.

By the end of the first year, I was completely confident in mathematics and the sciences. In my second year at Methody, I was taught physics by Marian Walton, daughter of Ernest Walton. Although I loved physics, I found myself increasingly drawn towards chemistry. In my final year at Down

High School, I had read Glenn T. Seaborg's *Elements of the Universe* (1958) and was fascinated by his account of the discovery of individual elements, as well as the capacity of the human mind to make sense of their often puzzling behaviour.

The great Russian chemist Dmitri Mendeleev had developed a 'Periodic Table of the Elements' (1869), which came to symbolise for me the way in which it was possible to discern a deeper structure and order within the world around us. Mendeleev arranged the chemical elements according to their properties, and found they fell into tabular form. At points, he proposed undiscovered elements to account for gaps in the table, and predicted what their chemical properties might be – predictions that were subsequently confirmed. What I found fascinating was that the awesome complexity and diversity of the real world – both the one I saw around me, and the fuzzy distant galaxies I could see faintly through my telescope – all emerged from the same hundred or so basic components that are woven together in endless forms in the fabric of the cosmos.

I found myself excited, sometimes even overwhelmed, by the ability of science to disclose the way our universe functioned, and the mysterious capacity of mathematics to represent these findings. Reading C.P. Snow's first novel one weekend in Methody's library reassured me that I was not alone here: Arthur Miles, its central character, tells of a physics lecturer at King's College London explaining Mendeleev's table of the elements in a manner that transformed the way in which he saw the world.

For the first time I saw a medley of haphazard facts fall into line and order. All the jumbles and recipes and hotchpotch of the inorganic chemistry of my boyhood seemed to fit into the scheme before my eyes – as though one were standing beside a jungle and it suddenly transformed itself into a Dutch garden. 'But it's true,' I said to myself. 'It's very beautiful. And it's true.'[1]

I didn't understand Snow's point about a 'Dutch garden', and had to consult an encyclopedia in the school library to find out that this referred to a formal organised garden, introduced into England in the seventeenth century by William of Orange. Snow saw this as a vivid way of visualising the order and structure that a successful theory brought to the sometimes chaotic 'jungle' of experience and observation. His words captured something that I had been trying to put into words for several months, with little success – the perception that scientific theories illuminate and organise the intellectual landscape. Such theories stripped away at least some of the masks and veils covering the surface of reality, allowing it to be seen for what it truly is.

Snow brought a growing precision to my still rather vague and unfocused thoughts about the virtues of theories in science. Shortly afterwards, I read Darwin's *Origin of Species*, noting his emphasis on how his theory of natural selection allowed certain otherwise puzzling observations – such as the persistence of nipples in male mammals – to be seen as an integral part of a greater coherent picture of the world. A good scientific theory allowed what might otherwise seem perplexing appear entirely reasonable, perhaps even predictable.

Although I could not match the verbal or imaginative brilliance of Snow, his comments offered me welcome intellectual reassurance that I had grasped at least something of what scientific theories were all about. A good theory enables us to see the coherence of reality, disclosing (not inventing) a fundamental interconnection of things which might otherwise be overlooked. It brings what seems to be a jungle into sharp focus, so that it appears as an ordered and elegant garden. But here was the point: if the theory is right, then our world *is* a garden, and not a jungle. The theory discloses order and elegance; it does not invent them, but rather gives the human mind a framework for perceiving them.

My study of chemistry helped me to see myself and the universe as made up of the same basic chemical elements. These were the building blocks of our cosmos, the letters in which its history was written and its nature disclosed. Yet while great literature is indeed written down in letters, the greatness of that literature does not lie in those characters printed on a page, but in the impact they have on their human readers as they grasp their significance and change the way they see themselves and the world. Knowing what I – and the universe – were made of did not even begin to answer my deeper questions about meaning and purpose.

I could hardly overlook the fact that scientific theories concerned our understanding of the fabric and functioning of the cosmos, not what they meant. They were morally and existentially agnostic – and rightly so. So did the inability of science to disclose values and meaning imply that people merely invented such notions, without any evidential basis? Or did this point to another angle of approach being required to disclose something that really was there, but did not show up on a scientific map of the cosmos? Did such ideas as 'meaning' simply slip through the net of the scientific method? Was science one tool among others, or the only reliable tool at our disposal? Was it a gateway to something richer, or was it complete in itself?

I found myself caught up in an internal struggle, with two very different ways of thinking competing for my loyalty. On the one hand was the view that science reveals a universe that we can understand, but that seemed to have no meaning. If this was so, it seemed that I had no option other than to face up to this bleak insight and get used to it. Only inadequate people needed to invent meaning as a way of coping with life. Strong people (among whom I somewhat immodestly numbered myself) were willing to embrace this absence of meaning boldly and defiantly, living without what Nietzsche described as 'metaphysical comfort'.

On the other hand, I regularly found myself challenged by what I would now call 'liminal experiences'. I often experienced a sense of standing on the threshold of some new world which beckoned to me, inviting me to enter even though it was not fully disclosed. A phrase from Pascal's *Pensées* seemed to capture my dilemma: 'the heart has its reasons'. My heart seemed to be drawn intuitively towards something that lay beyond my reason, as if it were a compass needle drawn to the magnetic north. But what should I make of these intuitions of my restless heart?

The first time I experienced this sense of standing on the brink of a world that was unknown to me was while I was reading a yellowed paperback edition of John Masters' novel *Coromandel!* (1955) at home during a school vacation. The novel tells of a mysterious map that led its hero on a journey of discovery to distant and exotic realms, initially for riches but ultimately for meaning. Whether Masters intended this or not, it spoke to me of a world beyond the horizons of my experience, and the need to find a map that charted the way to finding my heart's desire. If there was a road that led to that goal, I wanted to find it.

I also knew this feeling of awe and wonder from contemplating the solemn stillness of a star-studded night sky, which seemed to open my mind to grasping something deep and profound, even if this seemed to vanish like smoke when I tried to take hold of it. I found a perfect illustration of my situation in a woodcut, which I was told had been produced by some medieval artist, but which I later discovered dated from the late nineteenth century. It depicted someone rooted in the everyday world of experience being able to discern the deeper structures that lay behind it. I found it intriguing. Might nature be a gateway to a yet more wonderful world?

Woodcut from Camille Flammarion's
L'Atmosphère: Météorologie Populaire (Paris, 1888).

I had similar experiences when reading novels such as *The Coral Island*, or while examining my father's collection of postage stamps, which he began in the 1930s. The stamps bore the names of unknown realms that seemed to exude intrigue and mystery – Bermuda, the Cayman Islands and Fiji, for instance – and thus became windows to a wider and richer world beyond the realm of what I knew. I recognised the same sense of hovering tantalisingly on the brink of something unknown from looking at the night sky, and experiencing the silent and solemn beauty of the Pleiades in the constellation of Taurus. It was like looking through a dark window, seeing what lay beyond imperfectly – yet seeing enough to know there was something there worth pursuing. These experiences were important to me, making me receptive to deeper issues of meaning and value; yet I felt that they could not be given the same weight as scientific thinking. Science was objective; these experiences were decidedly subjective.

The more I understood about how our world functioned, though, the more pointless it seemed. The starlit heavens might indeed seem beautiful; they were, however, merely elegant symbols of cosmic meaninglessness and human insignificance. These thoughts, which I found simultaneously unsettling and exciting, were triggered especially by looking at a group of three stars at the centre of the constellation of Orion, a prominent feature of the Irish winter night sky. The textbooks I had read told me that those three stars – the 'Belt of Orion' – were so far removed from us that the light from the furthest took more than a thousand years to reach earth. I realised that I was seeing that star, not as it *was*, but as it *had been*, more than a millennium ago. Observing the night sky was, in effect, a form of time travel.

Alongside that undeniably intriguing insight, however, I found myself struggling to come to terms with the apparent insignificance of human beings in terms of the timescale of the universe. Some words from Tennyson's 'The Brook' seemed to express my feeling about this indifferent cosmos:

> For men may come and men may go
> But I go on for ever.

Initially, I saw the night sky simply as a thing of beauty and wonder, evoking awe on my part and creating a sense of longing to be initiated into its mysteries. This sense of wonder became a gateway for a desire to understand the universe – through reading, for example, Fred Hoyle's *Nature of the Universe* (1960). I could not, however, see the point of the universe. It simply existed. Like Joseph Conrad, I came to see 'dewy, clear, starry nights' as crushing our pride 'by the brilliant evidence of the awful loneliness, of the hopeless obscure insignificance of our globe lost in the splendid revelation of a glittering, soulless universe'.[2] I was nevertheless resistant to the idea that the physical immensity of the universe eliminated our significance as human beings, not least because we are able to conceive and grasp that immensity, and reflect on its implications for our meaning and value. What if meaning was not located within the universe, but in my decision to *create* that meaning – to choose to see the universe in a certain way? I, someone who had emerged from the fabric of the universe, could comprehend something of its complexity. Surely that was significant – at least for me?

Having completely failed to resolve these questions, I decided to set them to one side while I concentrated on my O Level examinations in June 1968. It proved much easier to focus on irregular French verbs than what I was coming to see as unanswerable questions about the meaning of life.

Later that summer, my mother drove me to Methody, where the examination results had been pasted on the windows of ground-floor classrooms, so that they were visible from the outside to our apprehensive eyes. My mother waited discreetly in the car while I, along with dozens of others, anxiously scanned the columns of print, wanting to find our names, yet not sure whether we really wanted to know the grades displayed alongside them.

I steeled myself; it was best to get this over as soon as possible. I discovered that I had passed English literature, English language and French with respectable grades. But more importantly, I realised with a sense of enormous relief that I would be able to enter the sixth form to specialise in mathematics and science. I had achieved top grades in every other paper.

3

A Sceptical Chemist

In September 1968 I returned to Methody as a sixth former. The expectation was that I would spend two years in the sixth form, and then go on to university – probably Queen's University Belfast – to study medicine or some medically related subject. The school's teaching timetable at A Level had limited flexibility, so that I was restricted in the subjects I could choose. Chemistry and physics were obvious choices, given my growing interest in 'hard' science, plus the fact that chemistry was seen as essential for most university courses in my field. But my decision to focus on physics meant that I would need a deep knowledge of mathematics, which demanded taking two papers in mathematics and further mathematics. I accepted with sadness that I would have to give up any hopes of studying biology at this level; I just couldn't fit it in. Happily (though perhaps surprisingly), most British university courses in medicine didn't require it.

It also meant that I would have no time for the serious studies of the humanities. Admittedly, I wasn't especially good at languages or literature, and knew my future did not lie in those directions. I nevertheless *enjoyed* these disciplines. I could see that they were important and enriching, and knew my specialisation in the narrow field of the hard sciences would impoverish me. I loved literature – and while I would still have time to read novels, I would not be able to study them at a scholarly level. Although Methody did not teach philosophy, its library allowed me to dabble in the field by reading introductory works, such as Norman Kemp Smith's *Philosophy of David Hume* (1941), as well as some Plato and Aristotle. At this stage, I saw philosophy as a critical tool to help me ask the right questions, rather than a privileged way of thinking that delivered the right answers.

Over the next year, for reasons that I still do not fully understand, I began to move firmly and decisively in an anti-religious direction. To begin with, I saw religion as unintelligible and unnecessary. I had nothing against it; like the universe, it simply seemed pointless. I could not see what difference accepting the existence of God made to my personal world. It was like discovering that there was an additional moon orbiting the planet Saturn: it might be vaguely interesting, but it made no obvious difference to life on earth.

I didn't see any need for a personal creed of any kind. The important thing was just to get on with life. Like the novelist E.M. Forster, though, I was aware that in rejecting other people's creeds I was in effect assuming a creed of my own. I solved this problem by limiting my creeds to factual and scientific – and hence epistemically safe – statements about the world. I knew I could be sure about these.

Atheism was, I came to believe, the natural resting place for a scientifically informed person. The natural sciences had expanded to fill the intellectual space once occupied by the now derelict and defunct idea of God. There was no need to propose, let alone take seriously, such an outmoded idea. I figured religion was a baleful relic of the past, revealed as a delusion by scientific advance. Surely Yuri Gagarin – the first human being to travel into space in April 1961 – was right when he was reported as quipping that there was no sign of any God up there. Perhaps I ought to have had doubts about the uncompromising bluntness of this pronouncement; yet it was what I wanted to hear – a scientific validation of what might have been little more than a personal prejudice or dislike on my part.

I can recall two landmarks along the road from religious indifference to outright hostility. The first was my reading of Bertrand Russell's *History of Western Philosophy*. Alarmed that my scientific focus was cutting me off from the humanities when I entered the sixth form, I made a point of reading widely in the school's library, and came across Russell's *History* in early 1969. It was here that I encountered the view that science and religion were at war with one another – the so-called 'conflict' or 'warfare' narrative.

Russell presented this as a plain and proven fact, illustrating it with a litany of disturbing historical narratives. For example, he pointed out that the sixteenth-century theologian John Calvin dismissed Copernicus' heliocentric theory of the solar system with a ridiculously simplistic appeal to the Bible.

> Calvin demolished Copernicus with the text: 'The world also is stablished, that it cannot be moved' (Psa. xciii.i), and exclaimed: 'Who will venture to place the authority of Copernicus above that of the Holy Spirit?'[1]

For Russell, this shocking historical fact was a telling and representative snapshot of a greater picture: the religious suppression of scientific advance, reflecting a deep clerical fear that science would expose and discredit the flimsy and flaky intellectual foundations of religion. The advance of science thus required the suppression, or at least the cultural marginalisation, of religion. I shared his indignation, and began to think in terms of the warfare of science and religion – a war from which I trusted science would emerge as victor.

The second landmark dated from August 1969, which saw the beginnings of what the Irish euphemistically refer to as 'the Troubles'. These were connected with – though distinct from – the general assault on the past that was so characteristic of the late 1960s. The ripples of the Paris student riots of May 1968 were felt by both students at Queen's University and sixth formers at Methody. The tectonic plates of the post-war age seemed to have permanently shifted, collapsing the cultural certainties of an older generation and creating a longing for radical social reconstruction by a younger generation. Student protests at Columbia University in New York, together with widespread discontent with the Vietnam War, hinted at a global restlessness, a Promethean urge to start all over again.

This seemingly global restive yearning for something new and better on the part of an alienated youth became locally entangled with something quite specific to Belfast – sectarian tensions, which erupted into violence in the summer of 1969. The sectarian conflict escalated, and the British Army was deployed to keep the peace. Although widely presented as fundamentally religious in motivation, 'the Troubles' were actually a political and ethnic conflict, reflecting two quite distinct sets of working-class beliefs and values. I chose to regard the religious aspect of the conflict as being determinative, in that it played into my solidifying perception that religion was a direct cause of violence. If there was no religion, I reasoned, there would be no religious violence.

Some radical students at Queen's University, just across the street from Methody, founded the 'People's Democracy' movement, which viewed 'the Troubles' through a radical socialist lens. (The People's Democracy fizzled out after a few years, torn apart by doctrinaire squabbles over Trotskyism, but I had by then moved on.) I got to know some of the people involved, including some former Methody students, and became interested in their commitment to Marxism as an ideology of liberation. This surprised me, given the violent Soviet suppression of the 'Prague Spring' of 1968, which my Czechoslovakian pen-friend of the time had described graphically to me. However, my friends insisted that this brutality represented a distortion of Marxism at the hands of Stalin and his successors. I was told that Theodore Adorno (a name that was new to me) had shown that students had a special role to play in advocating Marxism as a gospel of freedom. I decided this sounded appealing, and resolved to find out more about it.

The school library had a copy of Karl Marx's *Das Kapital*, which I duly began to read. After flicking my way through its seemingly endless prefaces, I began to read its opening analysis of 'commodities'. It was stunningly dull. Marx's lethargic prose having sucked the life out of my soul, I gave up this joyless experiment after twenty pages, wondering why anyone might find this interesting, let alone illuminating.

My experiment might have ended there, were it not that I had earlier read a study of the Manhattan Project – the American quest to create an atomic bomb during the Second World War. J. Robert Oppenheimer, whom many regarded as the mastermind of this project, died in 1967, prompting the publication of some assessments of his life and significance. I came across a phrase attributed to him in a newspaper interview, in which he declared that the best way to communicate something is to 'wrap it up in a person'. I wasn't entirely sure what Oppenheimer meant by this arresting statement, so chose to interpret it in my own way: 'If you want to understand something, ask someone who already knows about it to explain it to you.'

This suggested that I ought to consider a different strategy of exploration: talking to Marxists, rather than reading Marx. If I failed to grasp the significance of a writer or a way of thinking, I ought to listen to someone who had found them to be meaningful. This approach would allow me to grasp the core ideas of Marxism, as well as the grounds of its appeal. Objectively, I would be able to understand its ideas; subjectively, I would be able to appreciate the attraction of those ideas, and work out how they might secure traction in my own life.

It was not difficult to find some Queen's University students (including former Methody friends) who found Marxism compelling, and I happily listened to them explaining its theories over the greasy Formica tables of the nearby University Café, universally known as 'Smokey Joe's'. What I found especially interesting was the way they used these theories as a way of seeing and understanding the world, in order to be able to change it. Marx's theory was like a lens, which brought the world into focus, allowing you to see it as it really was – and thus to work out how to put it right. Just as Mendeleev had found a way of bringing theoretical order to the chemical elements, Marx had developed a theory that brought order and meaning to the historical process, enabling not so much its redirection as its acceleration towards its inevitable goal.

I began to grasp that Marxism wove together multiple strands of thought to yield a grand coherent way of understanding the world and acting within it. This was the first time I had come across the idea of a 'big picture' – a way of imagining or conceiving the world that allowed it to be seen as an integrated whole, rather than as a series of disconnected episodes or a patchwork of unrelated elements. Marxism offered a 'grand narrative', a script of human history which held together its apparently random and unpredictable twistings. It made sense – or so it seemed to me at the time – of the momentous events that were happening in the late 1960s, generating moral values and providing me with a place and a role within a greater scheme of things.

I had never come across such a way of thinking before, one that expanded my mind and subsequently left me dissatisfied with lesser and more limited theories that dealt with only individual aspects of our world and culture, but failed to connect them up into a coherent whole. Marxism, as it was presented to me by its youthful and enthusiastic advocates, was the only way of bringing together science, politics and ethics into an integrated whole, giving a grand and comprehensive – and hence *authoritative* – account of human life and thought.

I enjoyed hanging out with such radical thinkers at Queen's, and occasionally was able to slip away from Methody on Saturdays to attend their political meetings and screenings of some of the movies of Luis Buñuel. I found Marxism's comprehensiveness, weaving together the arts and sciences, to be intellectually exhilarating. Yet its chief virtue was that it gave me an intellectual justification for my growing alienation from religion. Marx's account of religion as an 'opium of the people' made sense of its social function, portraying it as an enemy to be subjugated, not an anomaly to be tolerated. It was a sedative, like opium, dulling our moral senses and thus making us lethargic and indifferent to the injustices of the world.

I particularly appreciated Marx's explanation of the origins of religion, which gave added intellectual weight to my increasingly trenchant atheism. At one student meeting, I learned that Marx based his criticism of religion on the avant-garde German philosopher Ludwig Feuerbach, who argued that God was an idea generated by the human mind to satisfy its longing for meaning and significance. God was thus not discovered, but *invented* to meet a specific need. Marx agreed with Feuerbach on this point, but was severely critical of Feuerbach for failing to point out that human longings were shaped by their social and economic context.

Religion thus arose to give human beings an 'illusory happiness' that helped them to cope with the miseries of life. Religion was indeed a narcotic, invented to enable people to soothe the pain of their journey through life, while at the same time allowing those in social control to manipulate them. But if our social and economic situation were to be changed for the better, the fundamental cause of religion would be eradicated. I learned to cherish Marx's criticism of Feuerbach: 'Philosophers have only interpreted the world, in various ways. The point, however, is to change it.'

If Marx was right about the causes of religion, it would simply disappear when a socialist revolution established a just society. The key to the elimination of religion, then, was social change. Marx's critique of religion thus had two core elements: a demonstration of its origins in social and economic alienation, and a prediction that a socialist revolution would lead to its natural disappearance.

Despite my deep rational attraction to Marxism, I was never politically active. While Marxism motivated others to radical social action, its impact on me was more intellectual than practical. Marx gave me a way of understanding why religion was so pervasive, demonstrating that it was merely a human invention arising from an existential need, and reassuring me that it would fade away in the future – despite its local cultural dominance in Belfast. I experienced a delicious, if smug, sense of enlightened superiority, being able to see why so many religious people around me were simply deluded. It was an inconvenient truth that some of them seemed to be rather better at science than I was – but I was sure that they would see the light in the end.

So, at the age of sixteen, I felt I had sorted out all the great questions of life in a way that resonated with my youthful intolerance of uncertainty and dislike of complexity. Marxism was demonstrably right – and hence so was my crystallising conviction of atheism. This alone was a thinking person's view of the world, devoid of the superstition, fables and fantasies of religious mythologies. It just remained to deal with one or two other issues – such as what I ought to do with the rest of my life. As it turned out, all these settled questions would have to be reviewed and revisited, as a series of unexpected developments unfolded.

4

Dreaming of Oxford

In September 1969, I returned to Methody for what I expected to be my final year, after which I would go to university. A decision was required: what would I study at university, and which university would I attend? There had been an expectation within the family that I would study medicine at Queen's University, following in my father's footsteps. My obvious growing interest in chemistry called this into question. While I might eventually become involved in medical research, it was becoming clear that I would be studying chemistry as a single specialist discipline – at least, to begin with.

I took my first A Level mathematics paper in the summer of 1969 at the age of sixteen and was awarded a grade A. This top grade would make it easy to gain admission to some of the country's best chemistry courses. My first choice was University College London, which had been highly recommended by some former Methody students. I was called for interview in late November, and flew from Belfast's Aldergrove Airport to London Heathrow, taking a bus from the airport to the centre of London, before walking to University College's Chemistry Department in Bloomsbury. The interview was perfunctory and uninteresting, but I was immediately offered a place there for the coming academic year, subject to a satisfactory performance in my three remaining A Level examination papers in the summer of 1970.

I should have been delighted. Yet seeds of doubt about my future plans had been planted weeks earlier by my conversations with David Wilson, an older fellow student at Methody whom I privately regarded as a rival but always valued as a friend. He had decided to study chemistry at Oxford, having concluded it offered the best chemistry course in the country. Why, he asked, wasn't I thinking of doing the same? He lent me his Oxford University prospectus, which provided details of its chemistry course, the college system, and the rich intellectual and cultural life that its students could expect to enjoy. I asked Dr Kenneth Reid, my chemistry teacher, for his advice. It was succinct and emphatic: I should apply to Oxford next time round. It would mean staying on for another year at Methody, as Oxford had its own entrance and scholarship examinations which took place in November. Rationally, I was persuaded. It made sense to go to Oxford. But would I be happy there? Would my heart follow where my reason pointed?

In December, David called me to tell me he had been awarded a scholarship to study chemistry at Oxford. Over tea at his house, he told me about his impressions of the city and university at his interview. It was like listening to a traveller's tale of old, conjuring up visions of an exotic and unknown world, remote from anything I had known or experienced. I began to sense a curiously intense longing, a desire for something that seemed to lie far beyond the boundaries of my experience yet promised a satisfaction that would be ample reward for its pursuit.

In the first week of January 1970, on a cold winter's night at home in Downpatrick, I dreamed of Oxford. I was walking slowly through its silent cobbled streets, steeped in history and scholarship, teeming with young people eagerly on their way to libraries or lecture theatres. As I passed by its elegant and ancient buildings, I found myself anxiously looking around me in case someone declared that I had no right to be there and asked me to leave. I feared being exposed as an impostor, a trespasser in the groves of Academe. I woke up, frightened, and wrapped a blanket around me for comfort as much as for warmth.

In a rare moment of insight, I realised that Oxford had become my heart's desire – something distant and possibly unattainable that I had come to see as immensely significant and personally transformative. In some way, the hope of going to Oxford had become part of me, whether I liked it or not. I could not understand why I experienced such a heartbreaking sense of longing to be somewhere that I did not even know. It was as if going to Oxford had become some sort of Platonic ideal, which chimed in with something deep within me that I did not properly know or understand. I wanted – no, I *yearned* – to belong there, yet feared that it lay tantalisingly beyond my reach.

Was this, I wondered, what religious people felt about God? Something that captured their hearts and imaginations, and not merely their minds? And did they experience that sickening fear of being denied entry to their paradise because they weren't good enough to be there? What if the hope of achieving my heart's desire was to be withdrawn? I felt a deep sense of separation from what I longed for, linked with a fear that this might become an unbridgeable chasm. I had finally seen what I really desired, while having to confront the fact that this paradise might lie beyond my abilities. I might see this city from afar, and yet find its doors barred to me.

In the cold depths of that night I worked out what I needed to do. Somehow, I was galvanised by setting myself what I knew might turn out to be an unattainable goal. Aiming for Oxford would test my limits to the utmost, allowing me to know myself through gaining a better sense of my own strengths and weaknesses. Seeing myself more reliably, stripping away any illusions about my abilities, might be a lesser goal than going to Oxford; it nevertheless seemed eminently worthwhile. I had nothing to lose by trying.

The next day, I explained to my parents that I had decided I ought to study chemistry at Oxford University. I would need to stay on for an additional four months at Methody to allow me to study for the Oxford entrance examinations. And if Oxford didn't work out, I would still be able to go to University College London, though a year later than I had originally intended. 'So what will you do after December?' My father was always practical. I knew that most of my friends who had applied to Oxford or Cambridge had left school at that point, and either found employment or travelled around Europe.

I had thought this through, though, and explained that I would like to stay on at Methody for the rest of the next academic year. I wanted to learn German and Russian, both of which would be useful for being able to read the scientific research literature (I didn't tell my parents that they would also come in useful in allowing me to read Marx, Engels and Lenin in their original languages). It would also allow me to focus on biology, which I loved, but had been unable to study at A Level at Methody because of other commitments. My parents withdrew to the kitchen to make a pot of tea. It seemed to take rather a long time to brew. On their eventual return, they brought tea, biscuits, and their support for my proposals for the next academic year.

Never one to leave things to chance, I began to plan a campaign of action. I would need to achieve top grades in my three remaining A Level examinations in the summer of 1970. Chemistry then had three main branches: organic, inorganic and physical. Although I loved all three, I was beginning to develop a fascination with inorganic chemistry, especially the way in which certain elements – like iron and magnesium – played such an important role in biological processes such as oxygen transport in blood and photosynthesis. I persuaded my parents to buy me Cotton and Wilkinson's *Advanced Inorganic Chemistry*, which came out in a second edition in 1966, as my birthday present. Dr Reid lent me his copy of another substantial work in the field – Phillip and Williams' *Inorganic Chemistry* (1965), which I found challenging and fascinating. In June 1970, I took my remaining three A Level examinations in further mathematics, chemistry and physics. To my immense relief, I obtained grade As in all three. The way was clear to apply to Oxford.

David Wilson had explained the admissions process to me. Oxford was a collegiate university. I would apply to one of the colleges that accepted undergraduates in chemistry. The college's tutors in chemistry would then interview me and decide whether I was up to their standards. If I was a borderline case, other colleges would be allowed to consider me. David had applied to St Edmund Hall, a college that traced its origins back to 1236. In the end, I chose to apply to Wadham College, founded in 1610. I knew nothing about it – except that the title page of Phillip and Williams' *Inorganic Chemistry* informed me that one of its authors, R.J.P. Williams, was based at Wadham College, Oxford. That was good enough for me.

I returned to Methody in September to prepare for the Oxford entrance examination. The school offered advanced teaching across the sciences and humanities for those preparing for the entrance examinations of both Oxford and Cambridge, allowing me individual specialist support in the fields of mathematics, physics and chemistry. I served as Head Boy of the Boarding Department, and Deputy Head Boy for the school as a whole – but these did not make significant demands on my time, leaving me ample space to focus on studying.

In early December, having taken the entrance examinations, I travelled to Oxford for interview, arriving at Wadham College late in the evening in the middle of a power cut. I was led through the darkness by the college porter, who guided me through shadowy ancient buildings, torch in hand, before leading me up a creaky wooden staircase to a student room that had been set aside for me. He gave me a letter that had arrived for me and told me that details of the time and place of my interview the following morning had been posted on the college noticeboard next to the main college entrance. He then disappeared, leaving me in complete darkness, unable even to read the letter he had given me.

Eventually, the college's power supply was restored, and I could study the letter I had received. It was from Dr Denis Meakins, the chemistry tutor at Keble College, inviting me to interview at his college the next afternoon. I mulled over its contents the following morning while playing around with the alarmingly greasy and undercooked fried egg I had been offered for breakfast in the college hall. I wasn't sure how to interpret this request from Keble. Did it mean that Wadham didn't want me, and so were allowing others to consider me instead?

Later that morning, I sat down on a dilapidated armchair outside the appointed room on the King's Arms staircase for my interview at Wadham. I could hear some voices inside, and caught fragments of their conversation. 'He got alpha minus in chemistry.' That didn't sound good to me, whatever it meant. 'Let's have him in.' The door opened, and a tall man resembling an eager gundog ushered me in, and introduced himself as Jeremy Knowles, the college's tutor in organic chemistry.

Knowles pointed to a chair where I was to sit, and then waved vaguely towards his two colleagues, whom he named as Stephen Simpson and Bob Williams. I instantly realised that 'Bob Williams' was the 'R.J.P. Williams' who had led me to apply to Wadham in the first place. 'So what do you find interesting about chemistry?' Knowles asked. I replied that I found inorganic chemistry fascinating. Knowles turned to Williams, and invited him to take over.

I was familiar with the word 'evisceration', but had rarely had cause to use it, or even to think about it. Yet that word describes precisely what happened next, as Williams probed my understanding of inorganic chemistry with relentless precision and depth. My every answer was parried with a more complex question, eventually leading us to a discussion of the Jahn–Teller effect, which stretched me to my absolute limits. I had no idea how long our discussion lasted, though I have a clear memory of how it ended. Williams leaned forward in his chair, pressing me on a point about transition metal ions. For the first time, I had to concede that I simply did not know the answer, although I offered him a speculative hypothesis in its place.[1] There followed a rather long and what I took to be ominous silence in which Williams stared at me, before Knowles stood up and told me they would be in touch in due course. The interview was over.

I walked back to my room somewhat despondently, convinced that I had ended any hope of coming to Oxford. After a disappointingly austere lunch, I walked the short distance to Keble College for my second interview. Denis Meakins and two colleagues – whose names I do not recall – probed my understanding of chemistry rigorously yet kindly, widening out the conversation to include more philosophical issues. My abiding memory of that interview was our discussion of whether Kant's philosophy was unduly dependent on Newton's notion of absolute space. While I left the room feeling this interview had gone well, I knew that it had lacked the conceptual depth of my earlier and more bruising encounter. It was polite, rather than penetrating.

I returned to Aldergrove late that evening, dreading the slow bus journey to Belfast, and the long, cold walk from Great Victoria Street Station to Methody. To my delight, I met a student friend in the arrivals area who had just returned from interview at Cambridge. He insisted that I joined him and his father, and allow them to drive me directly back to Methody. 'How did it go?' he asked, as we settled into their warm, comfortable car. I sighed. 'I don't really know.' A few days later, I went home for the Christmas holiday.

5

A Crisis of Faith

On Friday, 18 December 1970, I stumbled down the stairs from my bedroom to join my mother and sister for a late breakfast. I had been wondering when I would have any news from Oxford, and was expecting to hear something early the following week. None of my friends who had been interviewed for Oxford had heard anything yet, so I was not unduly concerned. Stanley Worrall had asked each of us to call him on his private home telephone as soon as we heard anything, in case he could be of any help.

After breakfast, I went for a walk to clear my head, following the Quoile downriver towards the Old Steamboat Quay, before returning to cross the river to walk along the Finnebrogue Road. When I returned an hour later, my mother told me that a Christmas card had arrived for me. I picked up the handwritten envelope lying on the kitchen table. As it was so close to Christmas, I assumed, like my mother, that it was a card from one of my friends. But I didn't recognise the handwriting. Then I noticed the postmark: Oxford.

This was definitely not a Christmas card. I sat down, and hesitantly opened the envelope, to find a terse, handwritten note from Jeremy Knowles, a mere two sentences long. I had been awarded a Major Scholarship at Wadham. Congratulations! My mother read the letter, puzzled. 'Does this mean you have a place at Oxford University?' she asked. I wasn't sure. Then I realised that my headmaster would be able to decipher the letter. Ten minutes later, I called Stanley Worrall at home.

Worrall was at his most genial. Yes, it meant that I had won a place at Oxford to read chemistry. In fact, I had done rather more than secure a place. I had won a scholarship that was not simply helpful financially; it was a mark of recognition. I would be going to Oxford singled out as one of its most talented new students. I struggled to take this in, as I felt I had performed badly at interview. Worrall laughed when I told him this, and explained that he had been expecting something like it. He had had a phone call from Dr Meakins at Keble, apologising that Keble would not be able to offer me a scholarship, as Wadham weren't going to release me to other colleges. Worrall assumed that this was because they wanted to offer me a scholarship themselves. He congratulated me, and told me he looked forward to seeing me around during the remainder of my final year at Methody.

Reassured, I explained to my mother what Knowles' letter meant. I had indeed gained a place at Oxford University. She called my father at work to explain this development, and on his return that evening, he brought out a rather old bottle of Asti Spumante which he was keeping for a special occasion. As nothing of great excitement had happened within our family for a few years, he decided this was probably the right time to open it. Drinking that lukewarm sparkling wine together remains one of my most vivid family memories from my time in Downpatrick. I still have the glasses we used on that occasion. The next day, I received a typewritten letter from Stuart Hampshire, the Warden of Wadham College, formally offering me a Major Scholarship in Natural Science.

So I returned to Methody in January 1971, free from any examination commitments, and able to devote six months of intense study to advanced biology, and learning German and Russian, making use of the college's excellent language teaching facilities (Methody was one of the few schools in Ireland to offer teaching in Russian). Dr Reid made me a present of his own copy of a textbook on 'scientific German', which helped me with the transition from everyday German to its more technical forms. I also had access to the resources of the school's specialist science library, as well as the larger collection of works in its main library, which allowed me to master the material I would have studied if I had taken an A Level paper in biology. Naturally, I continued to read about Marxism, consolidating my grasp of its core intellectual content, and expanding my understanding of its 'big picture' of reality.

Then things took an unexpected turn. After finishing my reading in biology, I started to explore other sections of the school science library. It had some rich pickings, including classics such as A.S. Eddington's *The Nature of the Physical World* (1928) and James Jeans' *Mysterious Universe* (1930). Having exhausted these, I came across a bookcase labelled 'The History and Philosophy of Science'. The accumulation of dust on its contents suggested it did not suffer unduly from frequent use. At this time, I regarded the history and philosophy of science as an area of study that amounted to little more than uninformed criticism of the certainties and simplicities of the natural sciences by those such as Karl Popper who felt threatened by them – what Richard Dawkins would later dismiss as 'truth-heckling'.

However, it seemed to me that intellectual integrity demanded that I explore its ideas, even if I was sure I would find them unpersuasive, even untenable. How could any serious empirical scientist, as I regarded myself to be, take seriously Karl Popper's suggestion that all scientific theories were conjectural rather than certain knowledge? I began with L.W. Hull's *History and Philosophy of Science: An Introduction* (1959), which offered a useful map of the territory I needed to investigate. I moved on to Arthur Koestler's *Ghost in the Machine* (1967), a rather more challenging work, calling into question just about every aspect of my scientific positivism. I read here arresting declarations such as the following: 'The progress of science is strewn, like an ancient desert trail, with the bleached skeletons of discarded theories which once seemed to possess eternal life'.[1]

Over the next weeks, it became clear to me why scientific positivists avoided engaging with the history and philosophy of science. If scientific theories that once commanded widespread support had now been displaced by superior alternatives, who could predict what would happen to these new theories in the future? The theories might be *better* than those they had supplanted; but did that mean that they were *right*? Might they not be transient staging-posts to something else, rather than final resting places? After all, the scientific consensus of the first decade of the twentieth century had been that the universe was more or less the same today as it always had been; yet this once fashionable and supposedly reliable view had been eclipsed by the seemingly unstoppable rise of the theory of cosmic origins generally known as the 'Big Bang'. (As I would later discover, Richard Dawkins' evasion of such issues, though rhetorically presented as a principled refusal to deal with anti-scientific wafflers, actually reflected the severe vulnerability of his approach at these critical points.)

I turned to Karl Popper, reading him closely and apprecia-tively, particularly his essay 'Science as Falsification' and his book *The Logic of Scientific Discovery* (1959). If Popper was right – or even partly right – I would have to come to terms with the awkward reality that all scientific knowledge is provisional, conjectural and hypothetical. We can never offer a decisive proof of our scientific theories.

I was experiencing an intellectual epiphany, and scales were falling from my eyes. Far from being ignorant sceptics who placed unnecessary obstacles in the relentless place of scientific advance, historians and philosophers of science asked all the right questions about the reliability and limits of scientific knowledge. And they were questions that I simply had not faced thus far. I was like a rather naive Christian who suddenly discovered that Jesus had not personally written the Apostles' Creed, or a flat-earther forced to come to terms with photographs of our planet taken from space.

It was as if the foundations of my world were being systematically dismantled. My simplistic view of science failed to take account of – to mention only a few of these formidable obstacles – the underdetermination of theory by data, radical theory-change in the history of science, and the difficulties in devising a 'crucial experiment'. In short, I realised that I had a shockingly naive view of science, which needed radical revision.

I was particularly disturbed by the arguments of the Victorian philosopher William Whewell, who suggested that any engagement with the natural world was shaped by pre-existing theories about nature. A 'mask of theory' always covers the face of nature. Whether consciously or not, we bring theoretical precommitments to our reading of nature.

For Whewell, this means that the distinction between facts and theories is deeply problematic – whereas I had thought it was straightforward and simple. What seems to be a fact from one perspective is a theory from another.

Having read Koestler's *Ghost in the Machine*, I went on to read his *Invisible Writing* (1954), in which he described his disillusionment with and intellectual alienation from Marxism. He once believed that Marx's theories allowed him to make sense of the world; its intellectual over-ambition, however, inevitably led it to force reality to fit its theories, and suppress other ways of understanding the world. And having abandoned this specific 'big picture', Koestler became sceptical about whether any such way of seeing the world actually existed, in that they offered only a 'specious clarity'. Where he once regarded the universe as an 'open book', he now saw it as a 'text written in invisible ink', allowing us at best to 'decipher a small fragment' of its complexity.[2]

Despite its unsettling consequences, I had enjoyed reading Koestler, and decided to keep going. I found a copy of his novel *Darkness at Noon* (1940), which depicted Stalinism in highly critical terms. I did not see this as a challenge to Marxism, taking the line that was common among students around that time – that Stalin had distorted the pure teachings of Marx. Nevertheless, Koestler raised the question of whether an atheist ideology could be at least as dogmatic as the Christianity it sought to displace. I was particularly drawn to his remark that 'revolutionary theory had frozen to a dogmatic cult, with a simplified, easily graspable catechism'.[3] I mentioned this to one of the Queen's University students with whom I had discussed Marxism earlier. He was dismissive of Koestler's *Darkness as Noon*, seeing it as intellectually lightweight – but not, he remarked, as ridiculous as Karl Popper's *Poverty of Historicism* (1957). I should stay clear of such revisionist nonsense.

Any freethinker like me would reach the same conclusion on hearing such words: why did my friend not want me to read Popper's *Poverty of Historicism*? What did it say that he found so threatening? Enjoying the lure of the forbidden, I found Popper's book in the college library, and began to read it. Its basic thesis, based on Popper's approach to the natural sciences, was that Marxism presented itself as a scientific theory – yet failed to be self-critical by making itself open to falsification. Marxism might assert the historical inevitability of socialism, but in fact this was little more than a hypothesis that had yet to be falsified. I could see why my friend had placed this work on his personal index of prohibited books. And I could also see that Popper had made some telling points – points that my friend did not want me to know about.

Popper was, of course, open to criticism here. Nevertheless he encouraged me to adopt a more critical attitude which marked the beginning of my process of disenchantment with Marxism, in which I moved away from seeing it as a normative 'big picture', and began to see it rather as a useful tool of cultural analysis, highlighting the influence of our social context on the way in which we think. It was thus a 'local picture', dealing with certain aspects of reality – but not all of them. But it also raised in my mind whether there was an alternative 'big picture' that I had yet to discover – perhaps lacking the over-ambition of Marxism, but nevertheless allowing me to grasp and express the fundamental coherence of things.

By the end of the summer of 1971, as I prepared go up

to Oxford, I was in a state of intellectual turmoil. I had experienced a crisis of faith, leading to the shattering of what I now realised to be spurious pseudo-certainties about the natural sciences. I found it difficult to cope with uncertainty, and had been drawn to both the natural sciences and Marxism precisely because I believed they offered the clarity and certainty I craved. Yet I was beginning to appreciate that I would have to come to terms with a lack of certainty about the really important things in life, which might lie beyond the kind of proof that the natural sciences or human logic might offer. Perhaps I ought to challenge my aversion to uncertainty, and temper this in the light of the realities of life.

This didn't mean I would believe anything I liked; it was simply an acknowledgement that I might only be able to prove shallow truths, not the ones that really mattered. Perhaps I had unwisely come to rely on an intuitive set of assumptions about belief, reason and proof that were much neater and more precise than the real world actually allowed. In my idealised world, there were clear demarcations between knowledge and belief; the real world, however, was irritatingly indistinct, offering a spectrum of possibilities. What could be known for certain seemed limited to logic and mathematics – a small and abstract world that was frustratingly disconnected from the debates and decisions of everyday life.

These deliberations did not directly call into question my atheism, or move me towards religious belief. They did, however, cause me to pause for thought. Why exactly had I embraced atheism? It was trendy. It irritated people I disliked. It seemed to be the way things were going. It resonated with my desire for autonomy. I wanted there to be no transcendent ground of being, so that I could do what I liked, instead of being obliged to act in accord with some greater and better good that was not of my own choosing or creating. Yet this seemed to be uncomfortably similar to Freud's idea of a 'wish-fulfilment', in which we invent a worldview that fits in with our tastes. Freud argued that we invent God to console ourselves. But what if I had invented atheism so I could be free of any interference or influence from some transcendent reality or ground, and thus be at liberty to behave as I pleased?

And what exactly were the objective *evidential* grounds of my atheism? I had dismissed religious faith because it could not be proved. But what if religion proved to be typical of our knowledge of reality, rather than the exception to it? If things that mattered lay beyond proof, *any* ethical, social or religious ideas counted as 'faith'. Even the idea that there is no God lay beyond proof. Was my atheism actually a faith – something that could not be proved, yet on which I took my stand? I was glad to be a freethinker, guided by my own reflections on the world, not any external authority. Yet my freethinking seemed to lead me directly into a place of confusion and uncertainty. Didn't Pascal say something about reason's final step being to demonstrate that many things lay beyond it?

I found a sentence in Russell's *History of Western Philosophy* that offered me hope, even if it understandably failed to deal fully with the unsettling questions I was confronting. 'To teach how to live without certainty, and yet without being paralyzed by hesitation, is perhaps the chief thing that philosophy, in our age, can still do for those who study it.'⁴ Russell seemed to be suggesting that I needed to challenge my obsessive quest for 'indubitable answers' to life's deepest questions. Perhaps, I told myself in a rather sermonising manner, I needed to challenge my inbuilt aversion to uncertainty. And maybe going to Oxford might help me find better answers to my questions than those I had yet encountered. It did.

6

Discovering God

In October 1971, I set out for Oxford, crossing the Irish Sea overnight on the *Ulster Queen*, and then heading south by rail from Liverpool to Oxford, changing trains at Birmingham New Street. I had spent the summer working as an administrative assistant in Downpatrick's local planning office, dealing with plans for new roads in the region, and was ready for a new challenge. In early September, Jeremy Knowles circulated some advice about preparing to study chemistry at Wadham, which made me wonder if I might have over-prepared for Oxford. Many of the first term's lecture and tutorial topics seemed to cover ground with which I was already familiar. Knowles' memorandum also introduced me to Oxford University's arcane names for its three eight-week teaching terms: Michaelmas (October to December), Hilary (January to March) and Trinity (April to June).

First-year chemistry students were required to take a specialist paper chosen from a limited number of options, one of which was quantum theory. This was a topic that I had not considered in any detail at Methody, and I knew it would be both demanding and exciting. It would be a gateway to the ideas of four German-speaking theorists whom I longed to understand: Werner Heisenberg, Max Planck, Erwin Schrödinger and the incomparable Albert Einstein. They did not disappoint, and I still continue to reflect on their ideas to this day. The basic Oxford lecture course on quantum theory was delivered with stunning clarity and panache by Dr Peter

Atkins, clearing away many of the obstacles I had encountered in understanding the field.

I had come to Oxford, however, not merely to climb a scientific mountain, but to sort out my jumbled and incoherent thoughts about the meaning of life. Reading Einstein in depth for the first time firmly persuaded me that science needed to be supplemented if it was to deal with the deepest human questions of meaning and value. It was an eye-opening and mind-expanding experience, which brought home to me with crystal clarity the need for a 'big picture' of reality that could hold together science, ethics and what Einstein termed 'religion' in a coherent whole.

Einstein's sense of 'rapturous amazement' at the natural world may have motivated his science, yet at the same time it heightened his belief that nature 'shows us only the lion's tail', pointing beyond itself to the majesty and grandeur of the magnificent animal to which it was attached – and to which it ultimately led.[1] Einstein confirmed my solidifying belief that, as human beings, we need more than a purely scientific account of the world. Yet he did not help me figure out how to move beyond this, even if it was helpful to have his support in acknowledging the limits of science.

At Oxford, I formed friendships with intelligent scientists – mostly chemists and physicists – who held a wide variety of political, moral and religious views, which they were able to defend rigorously. It gradually dawned on me that this diversity was more significant than I had appreciated. They were all scientists, but their scientific commitments and methods did not *determine* their politics, ethics or faith. Their shared love of science was matched by a diversity of moral and social values, from Marxism to free-market capitalism. My friends' religious views ranged from a committed atheism, through a cautious and principled agnosticism, to several forms of Christianity. These moral, social and religious ideas might be *informed* by their science, but they were certainly not *determined* by them. They were generated and sustained through different intellectual methods and criteria, adapted to the questions under discussion.

That said, I came across some students at Oxford, mainly on the fringes of serious science, who argued that *only* science could answer life's deepest questions. They held it to be self-evidently true that science had an exclusive intellectual privilege, in that it alone was able to demonstrate what was right; everything else was mere opinion or delusion. Not unreasonably, I invited them to prove this statement *scientifically*.

It was a perfectly legitimate request. If you assert that *A* is the only meaningful criterion of truth or assessment, your choice of that criterion can itself only be defended on the basis of *A* – which is viciously circular, in that the argument presupposes its own conclusions. Science, being uniquely and exclusively authoritative, thus confirms its own authority. And if we use other grounds to justify the authority of science, we are implicitly conceding the authority of something *beyond* science. The students whom I challenged on this point proved strikingly unable to get around this difficulty, although one of them ingeniously suggested the approach was *virtuously* circular, given that it was so obviously right. This blurring, or even denial, of the distinction between the premise and the conclusion of an argument left me intellectually baffled. Perhaps more importantly, it also left me existentially dissatisfied.

I fully accepted that science is a vitally important tool for investigating our world. Yet it illuminates only *part* of the picture, not the *whole* picture – and we need that grander vision of reality if we are to live authentic and meaningful lives, weaving together an objective scientific account of our world with our deepest existential needs, longings and aspirations. The natural sciences, rightly understood, do not restrict our study of this universe; they just help us work out what forms of research and knowledge count as 'scientific', conceding that there are other forms of investigation and knowledge that are not scientific – and are none the worse for that.

Although I was no longer a believing Marxist, I remained drawn to its idea of an underlying grand vision of reality. It was as if my mind, having been expanded by Marx's vision, protested against the lesser accounts of reality that I tried to put in its place. Something grander was called for. While Arthur Koestler seemed to have abandoned the idea of there being any such 'big picture' following his alienation from Marxism, I remained open to the possibility of an alternative, larger account of reality. I hoped to find some *Weltbild* – to borrow Einstein's term for a coherent way of perceiving the world – that would account for the successes of the sciences while at the same time identifying their limits, and help me weave together the objective and subjective aspects of life.

In my last few months at Methody, I had made a point of reading works of classical philosophy. By the time I had finished Aristotle's *Physics* and *Metaphysics*, I knew I had come across a serious natural philosopher whose ideas would continue to stimulate my own thinking. Plato seemed to me to be a less able philosopher, yet with a gift for using images that captured my imagination – the analogy of the cave in *The Republic* for instance. Plato here invites his readers to imagine a group of people, trapped in a dark underground cave for their entire lives, who know only a world of flickering shadows cast on the walls of the cave by a fire. In effect, Plato was conducting a 'thought-experiment', much like Einstein's famous image of riding a beam of light.

Such was the imaginative power of Plato's image that it transcended his original philosophical agenda, opening up new ways of seeing reality. Having experience of no other world, these prisoners assume that these shadows alone constitute reality. Yet the reader knows – and is meant to know – that there is another world beyond the cave, awaiting discovery. The cave does not define reality. As I read this passage, the hard-nosed rationalist within me smiled condescendingly at such a piece of escapist superstition. What you see is what you get, and there is nothing else to be said. But a still, small voice within me whispered words of doubt. What if this world is only *part* of the story? What if this world is only a shadowland? What if there is something more wonderful beyond it? And if there was, how could we know about it? And perhaps hope to enter it?

Although Plato's analogy seemed to point towards a religious way of thinking about things, I could not see how this had any connection with me. God was in heaven, wherever that was. But I existed in space and time. How could believing in God make any real difference to me, given the radical distance of God from my world, and God's total disconnection from that world? The whole religious enterprise appeared pointless. In any case, Christianity's vision of God – which was summed up in the seemingly nonsensical doctrine of the Trinity – was to all intents and purposes incorrigibly irrational, and was thus not a serious option for a thinking person like me.

However, there seemed to be something deeper within me that protested against this curt dismissal of faith. What if I had missed something? Might others have seen something that I had failed to grasp? After all, I had once been baffled by Marx's ideas, and had dealt with this by finding intelligent Marxists who could explain their beliefs, and help me grasp their significance. Yet I had conspicuously failed to have the same kind of explanatory conversations with religious believers, perhaps because I feared where these might take me. It now seemed to me that intellectual integrity demanded I listened to Christians, rather than arrogantly assuming I knew their beliefs better than they did.

There was no difficulty in finding such conversation partners. Oxford, as I soon discovered, was awash with highly intelligent science students who took their Christian faith very seriously, and made intellectual connections with their scientific disciplines. Even at Wadham, I knew physicists, chemists and mathematicians who had developed sophisticated accounts of their faith, and worked out ways of holding their religious faith and academic disciplines together. Some saw them as essentially different and unrelated aspects of their intellectual world, even though both were equally valued; others saw them as integrated elements of a principled quest for truth and meaning.

It soon became painfully clear to me that I had misunderstood what Christianity was all about. I had regarded it as a rather dull but respectable moral code commended and commanded by Jesus Christ, whose birth Christians marked at Christmas. My Christian friends spoke – though in various ways – of something rather different. They framed their faith in terms of discovering meaning and purpose within life. Faith, they assured me, was not about assent to the existence of an irrelevant God, but about the discovery and embrace of a transcendent reality underlying our world who could be *known* and *trusted*. Through many such conversations, I began to realise that I had carelessly and recklessly rejected a caricature of Christianity. I had not yet come to the conclusion that Christianity might be true or trustworthy; I had, however, certainly come to the conclusion that it was not what I had supposed it to be.

I was particularly challenged by my friends' accounts of how they understood the significance of Jesus Christ. Where I had thought of Christ as one of humanity's excessively numerous religious teachers, they talked about his significance in terms of 'incarnation' – a word that I had certainly heard, but whose significance had up to that point eluded me. This Christian term, I began to grasp, expressed the core belief that Jesus Christ *embodies* God. God is with us – not merely in the sense of being on our side but also in the sense of standing alongside us, sharing our story and journeying with us.

Before long, I realised that this specifically Christian idea of the incarnation was a game-changer. God – or at least the Christian God – was not a distant despot, who watched the sufferings of the world from a safe distance. *This* God chose to enter into this world, to share its pain and sorrow, to enter human history in human form, with all the risks this entailed. If this vision of God was right – and that, of course, remained to be explored – it would transform my understanding of the Christian God, and in doing so, remove a fundamental stumbling block to faith.

It would also cause a radical shift in the way in which I thought about Christ – no longer as a mere religious teacher, but as the embodiment of God in history, enabling God to be seen and known. I had not read the Bible with any inter-est or enthusiasm as a teenager, but I recalled something from the opening of the Gospel of John, which I now realise I had probably heard read at a Christmas service, perhaps at Methody: 'And the Word was made flesh, and dwelt among us' (John 1.14, KJV). Suddenly, I made a connection with Plato's cave. Christ was the one who entered into our cave, and led us to the better world beyond it, removing any barri-ers in our way.

It was an epiphanic moment, in which someone seemed to have switched on a light, allowing me to see things clearly, even luminously, for the first time. I had that sense again of standing on the threshold of a new way of thinking and living. I had glimpsed – but *only* glimpsed – something of what lay beyond, as if through darkened glass or a slightly out-of-focus lens. My imagination was captivated by this vision, able to see new connections and correlations that my reason struggled to grasp. It was not enough to persuade me rationally; yet a stronger force was at work within me, reach-ing out towards something that seemed able to hold together my mind and my heart.

What I had seen was enough. I wanted to enter and to belong, despite having unresolved questions and lingering anxieties. Would this be another dead end, like my flirtation with Marxism? Or might it be the beginning of something that would become a defining and permanent part of my life? There was only one way to find out. Taking a deep breath, I stepped across this threshold, and prepared to explore a strange new world that lay beyond.

PART TWO

An Unexpected Conversion:
Exploring a Strange New World

7

Shipwrecked on an Island of Faith

I returned home to Downpatrick at the beginning of December 1971 after my first term at Oxford, having spent a long, wintry night on the windswept deck of a ferry crossing the Irish Sea from Liverpool to Belfast, trying to make sense of what had happened to me. I had been told that Oxford changed people; yet I did not think it would change me in this way, or so soon. I loved science; yet my somewhat shaky scientific positivism had simply collapsed in the face of radical philosophical critiques and the brute facts of experience.

I still thought Marx was right about the influence of social location on the shaping of ideas; but I no longer accepted Marxism as a defining 'big picture' of the world. I was disturbed by its 'vaulting ambition, which o'erleaps itself.'[1] It was an intellectual Tower of Babel constructed on an inadequate foundation, whose only future was either total collapse or a radical contraction to something more realistic and limited. It seemed to me that Christianity had the capacity to offer a grander vision of our world, but this was still an intuition rather than a carefully reasoned conclusion. I had stepped into a new and strange realm, and felt a compulsion to explore its territory.

I did, of course, know something – though far less than I imagined – about Christianity, but began to appreciate that this somewhat meagre knowledge was mediated and unreliable. I was like someone who acquired a knowledge of

France through reading *Clochemerle*, or relied on Gilbert and Sullivan's *Mikado* in trying to understand Japanese culture. I would have to investigate this new world for myself, and not rely on secondhand accounts.

One of the books that captured my imagination as a child was R.M. Ballantyne's *Coral Island* (1858), a tale of three teenage boys who were shipwrecked on an uninhabited South Pacific island. I loved its evocative descriptions of the island's exotic landscape – such as its 'starry sky', 'gently rustling trees', and the sound of the 'distant roaring of the surf upon the coral reef'. The most enthralling aspect of Ballantyne's tale for me, however, was his account of the three teenagers' exploration of this strange new world, which helped them to grow as people.

I do not know quite how I made the connection, but as the ferry passed by the Isle of Man in the small hours of the morning on its way to Belfast, I figured that *The Coral Island* gave me an imaginative framework to reflect on where I now found myself. I had thought of my rationalism as being impregnable and invulnerable, an unsinkable ship like the *Titanic* (built in Belfast, close to where the ferry would dock in a few hours' time). Now I had been unexpectedly and inconveniently shipwrecked, thrown up on a beach strewn with the debris of my earlier rationalist certainties. But where had I landed? Could I survive here? There was only one way to find out: I would have to explore the island of faith properly. And, satisfied with that conclusion, I found a quiet corner inside the ship beside a broken slot machine, and fell asleep.

That task of exploration was conceived long ago in an instant of youthful imaginative interconnection on a dark night in the Irish Sea, in which insight seemed to leapfrog over rational dissection; yet it took forty years to implement, and it still continues. Ballantyne's *Coral Island* ends with a lyrical account of the three boys returning home, experiencing 'a thrill of joy, strangely mixed with sadness' as they gradually left behind them the 'beautiful, bright, green, coral islands of the Pacific Ocean'. The island had changed them; but it was not, and never would be, the place where they really belonged. I stayed on my adopted island, discovering its rich landscapes and hidden treasure, and learning from those who had already settled there. It became my home.

I began my journey into this new and unknown world with some trepidation. What was I to make of the seemingly impenetrable screen of thorny verbiage that surrounded the Christian faith – namely, its Creeds? These terse lists of apparently disconnected ideas failed either to capture my imagination or to illuminate my understanding. They seemed like a collection of neat little wooden boxes, which my lingering atheist prejudices led me to compare to coffins of a dead past. How could such dull verbal formulae encapsulate the bright vision of faith that so animated my Christian friends? I found a copy of the Church of Ireland's *Book of Common Prayer*, and stared at the text of the Apostles' Creed, hoping that its printed characters would somehow dissolve and rearrange themselves into something liberating, breathing and life-giving. Nothing of the sort happened.

On returning to Oxford in January 1972, I decided to follow a friend's advice, and read the Gospel according to Mark. I had taught myself Greek before going to Methody, working my way slowly and methodically through some basic Greek school textbooks dating from the 1920s, given to me by a great-uncle who was a Methodist minister. As I read the Greek text of Mark's Gospel, I was initially surprised by the simplicity of its language compared to the Attic Greek with which I was familiar. I then found myself lingering over the first words spoken by Christ in the narrative: 'The time is fulfilled, and the kingdom of God has drawn near; repent, and believe in the good news' (Mark 1.15).

The demand to 'repent' was familiar to me from the dreary billboards of street preachers in Belfast. I had, however, never given it much thought, tending to see this as preying on those with guilty consciences and being incomprehensible to everyone else. As I pondered the significance of the Greek word here translated as 'repent', though, I began to catch a glimpse of a new world that had up to this point eluded me. The Greek term *metanoia* did not naturally translate as 'repentance'; it rather designated a mental about-turn, an intellectual inversion, a radical changing of the way in which someone understands and envisages the world.

It was an idea that captured my imagination, particularly when I noticed that it recurred at every level of the New Testament: 'Do not be conformed to this world, but be transformed by the renewing of your minds' (Romans 12.2). The Christian gospel was an invitation to reimagine reality, to think in new and more expansive ways, to adopt a new imaginative template, to look through a telescope that would bring reality into sharper focus, showing the world as it really was.

I found this insight exciting. I had read a few works by the American novelist Henry Miller, enjoying his depiction of life as a chaotic and fragmented journey, in which our 'destination is never a place, but rather a new way of looking at things'.[2] Miller was an exotic nomad, whose travels in Greece on the eve of the Second World War, recounted in his rambling yet deeply evocative *Colossus of Maroussi* (1941), led to him 'opening his eyes' and 'expanding his whole being'. The whole point of journeying through life is to see the world in a new way. I realised that the Creeds were there to open my eyes and expand my vision, helping me to explore my faith by telling me what I should be looking for. They did not themselves *contain* this disclosure, but *mediated* it; they *pointed*, as if to say, 'See what there is to discover!'

I saw, for the first time, how I could understand – and perhaps more importantly, *use* – the Creeds. They were invitations to explore the Christian faith, and brief descriptions of what that process would allow me to discover. The Creeds were a gateway, a point of entry to a new world. They were a testimonial from the past concerning what had been found to be trustworthy and enlightening, a legacy of illumination and wisdom. The Creeds were like verbal maps of the landscape of faith, identifying landmarks to be encountered and appreciated in the journey of exploration and discovery. Their checklists would enable me to investigate this new landscape fully, without leaving anything out.

I had a second – perhaps more significant – concern however. I loved science, both in terms of its procedures and outcomes; yet I had been immersed in an intellectual subculture that insisted that science was incompatible with religious belief. I was blinded to alternative ways of thinking by a cultural accretion of prejudice and ridicule. My earlier atheism was enfolded in a protective accumulation of undisputed certainties, one of which was the inevitable and necessary warfare of science and faith. The spell of this rationalist incantation was partly broken by my many conversations with Oxford science students with religious convictions, who had found serviceable ways of reconciling them. But I was not entirely satisfied with what they offered me, namely what seemed to be intellectual workarounds, rather than intellectual solutions. I wanted something more rigorous and coherent.

I found the beginnings of a coherent answer a few months later in a sermon preached in Wadham College chapel by Charles A. Coulson, Oxford's first Professor of Theoretical Chemistry, and a Fellow of the College. Coulson was a prominent Methodist lay preacher, and author of the work *Science and Christian Belief* (1955). I had not read this book; indeed, I did not even know about it when Coulson preached on the fundamental coherence of the natural sciences and Christian faith. It was as if a light was turned on in the recesses of my mind that Sunday evening, allowing me to see the relation of science and faith in a new way.

Coulson's basic point was that science and religious faith offered different insights on understanding our world, reflecting their own distinct methods of approach. Science, faith and poetry represented distinct perspectives on a complex reality, which could not be limited or reduced to the insights gleaned from any single approach. It was like trying to describe a complex building, such as St Paul's Cathedral (designed by a former Wadham student, Christopher Wren). A total description of the building required the aggregation and integration of multiple perspectives. Its magnificent dome, chancel and crypt could be appreciated in their own right; yet each was an integral part of something greater. No single perspective was adequate to do justice to the totality of the cathedral's grandeur.

Afterwards, I was able to talk to Coulson about his sermon. We sat down beside a piano in the college's ante-chapel, as I explained my concerns. Coulson told me how he had shared similar questions while he was studying physics and mathematics at Cambridge in the 1930s. Coulson talked particularly about the rationality of faith, explaining that he believed in electrons not because he had personally observed them, but because proposing their existence made sense of a mass of apparently unrelated phenomena.

Coulson showed me that my new faith did not call upon me to abandon my love of the sciences, but to see science in a new way, which provided an additional motivation for loving science in the first place. I did not need to see my faith as conflicting with science, but as filling in the detail of a 'big picture' of which science was a major part – but *only* a part. Science was outstanding in its ability to help us understand how the universe functioned; it could not, however, disclose its meaning. From that point onwards, my intellectual exploration of the relation of science and faith was based on this simple generative insight.

Yet my conversation with Coulson was important in another way. He made it clear that he saw Christianity as offering a grand vision of life. He helped me to see that the intellectual appeal of Christianity to a scientist did not lie in the location of explanatory gaps that could be unconvincingly populated with a 'god'. Rather, Christianity articulated a rich and luminous, larger vision of an ordered world that was intelligible to a God-given mind, setting out a larger narrative that allowed me to engage with questions that were raised by science, yet which lay beyond its capacity to answer. Immediately, I made a connection: Christianity offered a 'big picture' of reality.

Coulson did not develop this point in our conversation, but it resonated with a well-known article of 1960 that I had read while researching quantum theory. The theoretical physicist Eugene Wigner pointed out in this article that science is constantly searching for the 'ultimate truth', which he defined as 'a picture which is a consistent fusion into a single unit of the little pictures, formed on the various aspects of nature'.[3] This idea of a 'big picture' integrating 'little pictures' caught my attention. It was like a panoramic view of a landscape, which was able to position and hold together snapshots of forests, rivers, roads and villages. These individual items belonged together in a greater coherent viewpoint.

Wigner's approach to 'ultimate truth' attracted me, although I could see an obvious downside – the dogmatism that seemed to accompany claims to have discovered such a total account of reality. I disliked dogmatism intensely, and admired some words attributed to Luis Buñuel that I had picked up from some Marxist friends at Queen's University: 'I would give my life for a man who is looking for the truth. But I would gladly kill a man who thinks that he has found the truth.' Would thinking I had found this truth make me intolerant and dogmatic, closing down my reflection and discussion? It was no idle fear. Totalising worldviews – such as Marxism and some fundamentalist forms of Christianity – showed an alarming tendency to see alternatives as enemies and threats which were to be resisted and ridiculed, rather than as enriching dialogue partners to be welcomed and engaged. As I later discovered, this was also true of the rather dogmatic forms of atheism found in the writings of Richard Dawkins and Christopher Hitchens.

While the risks of exclusivism and triumphalism could not be ignored, a 'big picture' of reality did not necessarily need to be intellectually imperialist. I could see how Christianity might offer a focused account of certain aspects of life, while leaving ample space for other aspects to be fleshed out using different methods of investigation. Christianity might be good on the question of the meaning of life; that did not suggest it could be relied upon to tell me the mean distance to the sun or the causes of the First World War. A 'big picture' could position major areas of human thought within its own framework, offering insights where appropriate, while treating them as autonomous areas of investigation. I had, however, little idea how this somewhat ambitious project might be developed. I stalled, unable to make progress.

In the meantime, I continued to exasperate my Christian friends with my endless questions on theological matters such as the doctrine of the Trinity. Eventually one of them, understandably wearied by my restless probing, told me that I needed to read C.S. Lewis to find some good answers. This was a name that meant little to me, although I had a hazy idea that he had written a book that had something to do with lions. Still, it was a constructive suggestion from someone I respected. In the middle of February 1974, I wandered into Blackwell's Bookshop on Broad Street, just around the corner from Wadham, and bought a book by Lewis using a book token sent to me a few weeks earlier by a relative as a birthday present. I had no idea of what the consequences of this simple step would be.

8

A Travelling Companion: C.S. Lewis

Looking back, I now wonder why I didn't discover C.S. Lewis much sooner than I did. After all, we were both born in Belfast, were fascinated with atheism as teenagers, and discovered Christianity at Oxford. Lewis' greatest works, in the views of both his admirers and critics, were *Mere Christianity* (1952) and *Surprised by Joy* (1955). I didn't know anything about Lewis when I visited Blackwell's Bookshop on that fateful day in February 1974, and wandered down to its subterranean Norrington Room, stacked high with books – including a selection of Lewis' works. In an untutored and uncritical way, I picked up a short collection of his essays, entitled *They Asked for a Paper* (1962). I took it back to Wadham as if it were a trophy of some great victory, and placed it alongside Jerry March's *Advanced Organic Chemistry* on the small section of a desk that I had commandeered as my personal space in Wadham College library.

I opened *They Asked for a Paper* and read the first essay – Lewis' inaugural lecture as Professor of Medieval and Renaissance English at Cambridge University. It was thought-provoking and remarkably well-written, but had little to say about Christianity, or the theological questions with which I was wrestling. Disappointed, I set the book to one side, and returned to annotating March.

A few days later, I found time to come back to *They Asked for a Paper*. I quickly decided that I could pass over Lewis' reflections on such matters as Hamlet and the 'Inner Ring' without significant loss, and moved immediately to the ninth essay in the collection, with the intriguing title 'Is Theology Poetry?' I didn't get any further for some time. After a furious flurry of annotation, especially of the final two pages of the essay, I knew I had found a travelling companion, someone whose forms of reasoning seemed to resonate with my own, yet whose conceptual grasp far exceeded mine, and whose writing style showed an elegance and sophistication that I could never hope to match.

I double-underscored the final sentence of that remarkable essay: 'I believe in Christianity as I believe that the Sun has risen, not only because I see it but because by it I see everything else.'[1] It was a moment of epiphany, of enlightenment and illumination. Someone else had seen with awesome clarity what I had merely glimpsed, and put this succinctly and memorably into words. I was no longer on my own. I had a travelling companion on my journey of exploration.

So what did I find in that essay, and why was it so important? Looking back, my concern had been that most of my scientist friends used a 'let's bolt it together somehow' approach to relate their science and faith. While I had nothing against this, I was searching for something deeper, which would provide me with a positive basis for the correlation of science and faith, rather than mere reasons for believing that they were not inconsistent. Lewis offered me a 'big picture' account of the Christian faith, which, though frustratingly vague on the particulars of individual sciences, located it meaningfully and plausibly within a coherent mental map of the world. The intellectual capaciousness of Christian theology was such that it could 'fit in' science, art, morality and other religious systems.

If Lewis was right, the multiple threads of our existence passed through the eye of a single needle, allowing us to grasp their interconnectedness and to bring them into a meaningful and potentially enriching dialogue. Where some saw life as a patchwork quilt of disconnected areas of existence and reflection – such as science, ethics, religion and art – Lewis argued that all were patterned together, woven into a more complex fabric that respected and retained their distinctive identities, yet revealed them to be part of a greater vision of reality. This did not represent an imperialist claim to cultural authority and intellectual supremacy (one of the more distasteful aspects of the Marxist ideology I had now left behind), but was rather a means of reassuring us of the possibility of living meaningfully within a complex yet ultimately coherent world.

Charles A. Coulson's insights on science and faith offering different perspectives on reality fitted easily within Lewis' greater scheme, while bringing greater specificity on the precise location of the natural sciences within this framework. Coulson was right in suggesting to me that I could not live with any kind of compartmentalisation of my mind, in which one hermetically sealed region was devoted to science, and another watertight compartment to my Christian faith. It was tempting to keep science and faith apart from each other; yet I felt that this amounted to an evasion of legitimate challenges that I would have to confront sooner or later. Intellectual integrity demanded that I had to find some way of allowing my love of science and my faith to interact, and to face up to the intellectual questions that this rightly raised. Lewis gave me the framework I needed to make this possible.

This single essay, 'Is Theology Poetry?', transformed my understanding of Christianity from a loose aggregation of essentially disconnected ideas – which is how I then understood the Creeds – into a coherent vision of reality, weaving together its threads to reveal a pattern. No matter how fragmented our experience of the world may seem at times, Lewis holds that there is a 'big picture' that allows things to be seen as interconnected. This theme is clearly articulated in the New Testament, which speaks of all things 'holding together' or being 'knit together' in Christ (Colossians 1.17). Christianity is not, however, about the discovery of an abstract and impersonal pattern, but the disclosure of this pattern in a person, providing a firm conceptual link between *understanding* our history and a transformative and illuminative moment *in* that history, in which 'the Word became flesh and lived among us' (John 1.14).

There was more to find in the final four essays in that volume of papers. Indeed, Lewis had kept the best wine until the end.[2] His essay 'On Obstinacy in Belief' helped me understand why I had been so drawn to atheism as a teenager. Lewis' discussion of the 'doctrine of the concealed wish' helped me see that I resisted belief in God partly because of the 'universal pressure of the wish that God should not exist'. Atheism, for Lewis, was to be seen as 'an admirable gratification to one of our strongest suppressed wishes' – the desire for total autonomy, and a freedom to pursue only what suited us.[3] Had I, as Lewis suggested, been led to atheism by my desires, and then 'produced the arguments afterwards as a rationalisation' of those desires?

If Lewis was right, my earlier desire to be a freethinker had become entangled with a shallow and uncritical rejection of any authority beyond myself – an aspiration expressed neatly in William Ernest Henley's poem *Invictus* (1875):

I am the master of my fate,
I am the captain of my soul.

My atheism was only one element of a self-serving and self-referential intellectual world that I had constructed, which was comprehensively dismantled by the New Testament's emphasis on discarding an old self-centred nature, and being transformed to something new, alive and alert to greater transforming realities (Ephesians 2.22–4). Such thoughts had passed through my mind while I was at Methody, but I had not been able to articulate them clearly, or locate them within a wider context.

In Lewis, I found the intelligent and winsome exposition of Christianity that I had longed for but failed to locate up to that point. The clarity and comprehensiveness of Lewis' vision of Christianity was, however, clearly shaped by and grounded in a profound immersion in the depths of a tradition of thought that I had not encountered. Lewis persuaded me, by the quality as much as the substance of his arguments, that I would have to study Christian theology in detail if I was going to have the intellectual toolkit necessary for the meaningful inhabitation and scholarly exploration of the borderlands of science and faith. The only way I could see of doing this was by taking a theology degree at Oxford, which would ensure that I was taught personally by leading authorities in the subject. Yet I could envisage no way of achieving this. It would require time and funds that I did not have, and could not hope to have. Lewis had created a frustratingly persistent desire within me that seemed to lie beyond any hope of fulfilment.

While I was dreaming of theology, though, I was still studying chemistry, and had things to sort out in the real world.

Jeremy Knowles asked me to see him in the last week of Hilary Term 1974 to discuss what I would be doing in the fourth and final year of my chemistry degree. Oxford's chemistry course then consisted of two parts: a three-year taught component, culminating in Final Examinations at the end of the third year, followed by a year's research work in an Oxford laboratory, leading to the production of a short thesis. I had already given some thought to this question, and considered a number of options tentatively. While I remained fascinated by quantum theory, and had once thought of researching Heisenberg's 'uncertainty theory', I was becoming more interested in complex biological systems, and wanted to research some of their chemical aspects.

Oxford was traditionally lubricated by sherry in those days, and Knowles poured us both rather large glasses to stimulate our discussion. He began by quizzing me about what aspects of chemistry I found most compelling. I told him about my growing interest in the chemistry of biological systems, particularly the recently developed Fluid Mosaic Model of biological membranes. I could see ways in which I could bring chemical perspectives to the study of such biological structures. Was this a possible Part Two project?

Knowles steepled his hands and looked at the ceiling for a few moments, before asking me if I had met George Radda, a Hungarian biochemist who had escaped from his native land following the Soviet invasion of 1956. Radda had made his way to England, taught himself English, and studied chemistry at Oxford. He and Knowles had both undertaken their doctoral research in the Oxford laboratory of Sir Richard Norman in the early 1960s. Radda now directed a large research group in the Department of Biochemistry, and had recently become increasingly interested in using physical chemical methods for investigating biological systems, particularly biological membranes. In Knowles' view, the fit could not be better. We agreed that I ought to apply immediately to work in Radda's laboratory for my Part Two – and make sure I secured First Class honours in the summer of 1974, so that I could do doctoral work afterwards.

That matter having been settled, Knowles asked me how I was finding the chemistry course. Was it fulfilling my expectations? Happily, I was able to report that I was finding organic chemistry – Knowles' own field – especially stimulating at that point, having read much of the recent research literature concerning the E_1cB elimination reaction mechanism. While the details of this reaction mechanism are irrelevant to this narrative, I mentioned that I thought I could see a way of making sense of an anomaly that I had noted in the research literature. Knowles pricked up his ears. 'That sounds interesting. Write it up!'

I then broached the delicate subject of changing academic direction. I explained, almost apologetically, that I was becoming interested in theology – a subject that Wadham did not teach – and was thinking of giving up chemistry in order to study this in detail. I stressed how much I loved chemistry, but was beginning to realise that I wanted to set this in a wider context. Knowles remarked that he knew some people who had done something like this in the past, his tone suggesting that he considered them to have fallen from grace. Had I thought this through properly? I conceded I had not given it detailed consideration. It was only a possibility, which was why I was asking him for his advice.

Knowles sat frowning in silence for a moment, then told me that I had to 'stoke the intellectual fires within me', and mentioned his own interdisciplinary interests, including a well-concealed passion for Mozart. Knowles then expressed what he considered to be a fundamental and legitimate concern: that in trying to do two things, I would do them both badly. Drawing somewhat freely on the metaphor of the hedgehog and the fox, attributed to the Greek poet Archilochus, Knowles explained that he saw himself as a hedgehog – someone who developed a deep understanding of a small area of the intellectual landscape. He was worried that I would become a fox, covering a much greater area of intellectual territory, but in a rather superficial way.

Knowles suggested that my credibility as a serious partici-ant in any dialogue between science and theology – which he assumed was my goal – would rest on having depth in both fields. That meant that I had to gain a doctorate in a mainline natural science in the first place, and some publi-cations in the field in the second. If I really wanted to move into the study of theology, he hoped I would stay in the scientific field until I had secured those two goals. He expected that I would need to do the same in theology. In the meantime, Knowles asked me to postpone any such radical decision until it became clear how well I had performed in the Final Examinations that summer.

It was a helpful conversation, and I was happy with its outcomes. I wrote to Radda, as Knowles suggested, and waited to hear from him. Meanwhile, Wadham College announced an essay competition for its undergraduates, who were invited to submit original pieces of research in any field of study for a College Essay Prize. Up to three prizes of £20 would be awarded. I read the notice with interest. Why not write up my ideas about the E1cB elimination reaction mechanism for this purpose? It would help me clarify my thoughts, even if it came to nothing. I duly wrote the paper, submitted it, and forgot about it.

In the final week of May, I found two letters waiting for me in Wadham's porters' lodge. One was from Stuart Hampshire congratulating me on my Prize Essay, and informing me I had been awarded one of the £20 prizes. The second was from George Radda, telling me that he would be pleased for me to join his research group in the Department of Biochemistry in September. I felt I deserved a celebratory cup of tea in the Junior Common Room bar, before going back to revise in the library for the rest of the day.

My Final Examinations, held shortly afterwards at the Examination Schools on the High Street, were spread out over several days. I found the ritual of dressing in subfusc – Oxford's formal academic attire, worn for academic examinations – sobering, helping me to cope with the stress of the occasion as I walked with my fellow chemists from Wadham down to join more than two hundred others at the Examination Schools. My chief memory of those Finals was walking back to Wadham during a torrential thunderstorm after an afternoon examination.

So I returned to Downpatrick for the summer vacation. There was nothing I could do at home in preparation for working with George Radda in the Department of Biochemistry. I would have to wait to find out how well I had done in the examinations, and hope that my performance would be strong enough to allow me to continue to work with Radda at doctoral level. This allowed me some guiltless time for reading and annotating the books by C.S. Lewis that I had bought with my £20 College Essay Prize.

Finally, a letter arrived from Knowles in the middle of July. By now, I knew his handwriting, and had no doubt that he had written to convey news of my examination results, and perhaps to offer his assessment of my prospects. Knowles was brief, and to the point. My results placed me in the middle of the First Class. I needed to make sure that my Part Two thesis was at least as good as my performance in the written examinations – and if this was the case, I would be awarded First Class honours in the summer of 1975. He wished me well for my future (he placed what I trusted was a kindly exclamation mark in parentheses after that word).

Knowles' letter brought relief, but also a degree of sadness. Knowles was leaving Oxford the following month to take up a Professorship in Chemistry at Harvard University. He had been something of a mentor to me, and I had taken some of his ideas to heart, above all, the need for depth in my studies. I took comfort from the final words of the letter, in which Knowles expressed the hope we would meet again. I spent August with my family, then headed back to Oxford to begin the next phase of my life.

9

The First Mountain: Science

On a beautiful early autumn morning in late September 1974, I made my way to Oxford University's Department of Biochemistry for my first meeting with George Radda. At that time, Oxford's busy and sprawling Department of Biochemistry was based in two adjacent buildings: the two-story Rudolf Peters Building, dating from the 1920s, and the massive eight-story Hans Krebs Building, built in 1964, which was then the highest (and possibly the ugliest) building in Oxford. A kindly receptionist showed me to Radda's office on the ground floor of the Peters Building. Radda was a genial and beaming figure in the midst of a scene of organised chaos, with research papers, typescripts of articles and scientific journals stacked on desks. I instantly liked him.

After welcoming me, he reached for a photocopy of a recent journal article dealing with the phenomenon of excited state proton transfer. He explained that the basic idea was that when certain molecules – such as derivatives of anthracene – were excited with ultraviolet radiation, they altered their acidity characteristics. These changes could be studied using fluorescence spectroscopy and had significant potential for developing chemical probes that could be used to explore certain important biological processes. (Fluorescence is the phenomenon in which certain molecules absorb high frequency ultraviolet light, and re-emit it at a lower frequency – typically appearing blue.)

Radda wanted me to extend this approach, using sophisticated technology that he had acquired for another research project, which allowed the changed characteristics of such molecules to be studied over very short time frames, measured in nanoseconds – that is, in thousand-millionths of a second. He invited me to come back and see him again later that afternoon, once I had been able to read and digest the paper.

Wadham College was only five minutes' walk from the laboratory. I found a comfortable armchair in the Middle Common Room, made myself a cup of coffee, and settled down to read the article and take notes. After an hour or so, I could see that Radda had given me a superb project – self-contained and manageable, yet capable of being extended if certain lines of investigation worked out. All I needed to do was become familiar with the technology I would have to use, devise some experiments, and develop some mathematical models to interpret the results.

I returned to see Radda again that afternoon, and thanked him for devising what looked like a remarkably interesting project. He beamed. 'I knew you would like it!' He then introduced me to people working in the laboratory next to his office in the Peters Building, before taking me to the laboratory where I would be based, on the third floor of the Krebs Building. It was a small room, with a large laboratory bench running down its centre. I was allocated half of one side of this bench; the other half would be occupied by another Part Two chemistry student, who would be arriving later that week.

Radda explained that the other side of the room, packed full of electronic equipment, was where one of his postdoctoral research students worked. Radda then led me back to his office, and asked one of his research students to help me get set up the next morning. I needed to discover the procedures for booking equipment, ordering chemicals and programming the laboratory's only computer, a Digital Equipment Corporation PDP-11 with one kilobyte of memory.

I soon settled into a regular routine, arriving in the laboratory at about 9.00 a.m., and working through to 6.00 p.m. when I had evening engagements, and to 10.00 p.m. when I did not. I didn't work at weekends that first term, so that I could socialise on Saturdays, and go to church on Sundays. I attended Wadham College chapel on Sunday evenings, and usually went to one of the large city-centre churches – St Ebbe's or St Aldate's – on Sunday mornings. Their sermons tended to be practical and devotional, so never really addressed the intellectual issues that I wanted to explore. I began to attend Pusey House occasionally, as its sermons were much more intellectual, and often touched on themes that I hoped to explore further.

Radda was an excellent supervisor and a highly effective leader of his research group. He appreciated the importance of assembling a group of researchers with multiple skills – such as experience with nuclear magnetic resonance and electron spin resonance – and encouraging new initiatives within the group that exploited this rich skill base. Radda did much to foster a sense of group identity and solidarity within the group. We met every morning for coffee, once a week for progress reports and seminars on work being undertaken within the group, and occasionally late in the afternoon to celebrate successes – such as the award of grants or prizes, securing a new academic position, or completing a doctorate. The top shelves against one of the laboratory's walls were occupied by empty champagne bottles, each with a brief inscription to remind the group of the occasion they marked. Radda's group was very successful, and there were many such celebrations, each with its own commemorative bottle.

My research went remarkably well, mainly because of Radda's shrewd perception of the significance of excited state proton transfer. By the end of Michaelmas Term 1974 I had a solid base of experimental results that proved to be theoretically significant. I would need to do more work to establish some secure links with biological systems, but could see ways of doing that. I began to wonder what I should do with what seemed to be a vast expanse of uncommitted research time that lay ahead over the next two terms.

I first met Radda's postdoctoral fellow Chris Morgan late one afternoon a few weeks after my arrival, when he stumbled into the laboratory, smoking a cigarette and using a nearby Petri dish as an ashtray. I wandered round to his side of the bench and introduced myself, telling him a little about the project I was working on. He liked it, and told me about his own work on developing a fluorescence spectrometer that could deliver real-time analysis of the polarisation of the light emitted from fluorescent probes in models of biological membranes. The extent of the polarisation of the light was a measure of the freedom of the fluorescent molecule to rotate, and thus provided a tool to determine the fluidity of the membrane under varying conditions. There were problems with the approach, however, and Morgan was researching how these fluorescent probes could be used in a more sophisticated way. Since there was some overlap with my own studies, it was natural for us to compare notes.

Late in December 1974, Morgan and I came up with an idea, which I shall try to explain as simply as possible. The fluorescent probe that Morgan was using for his experiments was based on a derivative of anthracene.[1] As a chemist, I knew that anthracene underwent a curious reaction when exposed to very high intensity ultraviolet light: two molecules of anthracene would combine to form a single molecule – a 'dimer' known as dianthracene. So might Morgan's fluorescent probe undergo this same reaction? And if so, could we use the rate of this process of 'photo-dimerization' to measure fluidity in biological membranes?

We began work immediately, and quickly found that the derivative of anthracene used in Morgan's fluorescent probe did indeed dimerize when exposed to high intensity ultraviolet light. Since the resulting dimer was not fluorescent, we could use the diminishing intensity of the probe's emitted light as a measure of the extent of its dimerization. In early January 1975, after the Christmas break, we tracked the rate of dimerization of the probe in a range of solvents, and were able to correlate this directly with their viscosity. We then implanted this fluorescent probe in models of biological membranes, and found that the same process of photodimerization took place in that context as well. Finally, we borrowed some live biological membranes from other members of Radda's research group, and observed the same pattern. We realised we had a new way of measuring the fluidity of biological membranes, which correlated well with the results of other approaches. Yet it also disclosed that these probes seemed to be clustered, rather than being distributed uniformly throughout the system being investigated. This had important implications for the interpretation of earlier results based on these probes.

Late in January, we went to Radda, and explained why this new approach had such potential. Radda came up to our laboratory, and we talked him through the experiments, including a real-time demonstration of the effect in biological membranes. Radda told us to write it up for publication in *Biochimica et Biophysica Acta*. It was accepted for publication with a minor amendment concerning our formulae for the calculation of lipid viscosity. I was now in the unusual position of having had a research paper accepted for publication while I was still an undergraduate.[2]

In the middle of February, Radda wandered into my laboratory, and asked me to explain to him exactly where I was with my Part Two research on excited state proton transfer. I explained what I had achieved to date, noting that the project was more or less complete. I asked Radda how I should include my new research on photodimerization into my Part Two thesis. It didn't seem to fit in very well with my work on proton transfer, and I was worried that the examiners might think the thesis was conceptually incoherent.

Radda told me that I had totally failed to grasp the situation. My work on excited state proton transfer was already good enough to secure First Class honours in chemistry that summer, given my strong performance earlier. The work on photodimerization would not be included in my Part Two thesis; it would serve as the basis of my doctoral thesis. (Oxford used – and still uses – the abbreviation 'DPhil' rather than the more familiar 'PhD'.) I had, in effect, begun my doctoral research eight months earlier than anyone had expected.

Radda then told me that Linacre College – one of Oxford's few graduate colleges – had advertised an E.P. Abraham Cephalosporin Studentship for research in the biological, medical or chemical sciences, which would cover all the fees and living costs of my doctoral research for at least two, and probably three, years. Would I please apply for this? The deadline was 1 March. I duly sent off an application, highlighting – at Radda's suggestion – my recent work on photodimerization. I was called for interview at Linacre in the middle of May, and shortly afterwards Renford Bambrough, the Principal of the college, wrote to tell me I had been elected to the E.P. Abraham Cephalosporin Studentship, on condition that I was awarded First or Second Class honours. Another commemorative bottle was duly added to the laboratory's shelves.

My research now shifted direction. I tied up all the loose ends of my work on excited state proton transfer, and wrote it up as my Part Two thesis. Chris Morgan and I began a detailed plan of research on how we might develop and extend our work on photodimerization. I spent only two weeks at home that summer, because I was so busy developing new research projects. As it happened, I was at home in the middle of July when a letter arrived from John Brown, Jeremy Knowles' successor as Tutor in Organic Chemistry at Wadham, telling me I had been awarded First Class honours in Chemistry. This was followed by a handwritten letter from Stuart Hampshire, congratulating me and wishing me well in the future.

So in September 1975, I left Wadham to become a graduate student at Linacre College, then located beside the Oxford City Police Station in St Aldate's. I moved from a student room in Marston to accommodation in Warnborough Road, an easy walk from the Department of Biochemistry. I was so busy in the laboratory that I did not have enough time to get involved in college events. Chris Morgan and I worked together on developing further substantial projects, including applying the phenomenon of condensed phase scintillation to biological systems, and what we believed was the first application of positron emission to the study of biological membranes.

The demands of my research in the Michaelmas Term of 1975 were so great that I had little opportunity for theological reading. I bided my time; I had got a lot out of C.S. Lewis, having progressed to his two substantial works *Mere Christianity* and *Surprised by Joy*, and was perfectly happy to wait before beginning my exploration of my faith more rigorously. Since Linacre had neither chapel nor chaplain, I continued to attend Wadham College chapel, and became friends with its new chaplain, Tim Gorringe, who had previously worked in a parish in Leeds. Gorringe was interested in the Swiss theologian Karl Barth, and proved an invaluable conversation partner, making me long to be able to study theology properly, even though I was by now reconciled to this being a remote possibility. Barth's writing style struck me as rather less engaging than C.S. Lewis'; yet his articulation of the nature and tasks of theology seemed intellectually compelling.

In the first week of December 1975, Radda wandered into my laboratory again, a copy of the *University Gazette* in hand, opened at a page of the 'Appointments' section that he had circled in thick black ink. Merton College was offering up to three Senior Scholarships to support research in any subject; and Christ Church was offering one Senior Scholarship, again without restriction on subject. These were *very* significant awards, Radda told me, with substantial reputational payloads. There would be massive competition for them, but he felt I was in a good position to get one and encouraged me to apply for both.

The deadlines were not until the middle of January, so I had plenty of time to prepare. I read the details, noting with interest that, in addition to covering all university fees, both offered free accommodation in college, as well as limited dining rights on High Table. It was not a difficult decision. I applied and was shortlisted for both.

My first interview was on Wednesday, 25 February at Merton College, founded in 1264. I had never visited the College before, and decided to arrive early, partly to steady my nerves, but mainly to get a sense of what it was like. I walked around its beautiful gardens, admired the views to the south across the expanses of Christ Church Meadow, and explored its medieval chapel. Something deep within told me that this might be the right place for me. I knew that Merton, however, might not share my view on this matter.

The interview, I remember, took place at 4.40 p.m. in the Senior Common Room. I had expected to face a small panel – as I had when I was interviewed nine months earlier for the Linacre studentship. The room, however, was packed with dons. They laid into me with enthusiasm, probing my research in depth with a critical acumen that reminded me of my earlier encounter with R.J.P. Williams back in December 1970. After tearing me to pieces, they thanked me for coming to see them, and told me they would be in touch in due course. I left the college wondering if I would ever see it again. It seemed like a wonderful place, steeped in history and learning. I tried not to think too much about this, and went to have dinner that evening with David Wilson, who was then working for the Atomic Energy Research Establishment at nearby Harwell. He brought me down to earth by telling me about his work on the disposal of hazardous radioactive waste.

My interview at Christ Church was set for 3.15 p.m. on the afternoon of Saturday, 28 February in the College's

Senior Common Room dining room in Tom Quad. It was not difficult to see ways in which I could learn from my Merton experience, and I was confident that I would be better prepared for this second interview. But it never happened.

Late on the afternoon of Thursday, 26 February, as I was passing the Department of Biochemistry's glass-fronted administrative office, one of the secretaries saw me, and ran out to tell me that Merton College were on the telephone, and they wanted to speak to me urgently. I went into the office and took the call. I cannot remember who I was speaking to, but I shall never forget the substance of the call. If I was offered a Senior Scholarship at Merton, would I accept it? I took a deep breath and said I would. I was told that I would receive a formal offer letter the next day.

My anxiety levels were such that the next day seemed to take an extraordinarily long time to arrive. Shortly after lunch, I received the promised letter formally offering me the Senior Scholarship and asking for an immediate reply in writing confirming that I would accept. I wrote to Merton accepting the scholarship, and then composed a somewhat apologetic letter to Henry Chadwick, Dean of Christ Church, explaining that I would have to withdraw from my interview on Saturday, as I had been offered a comparable position elsewhere. Having done this, I walked down to the two colleges – which are very close to each other – and delivered both letters by hand.

Radda was delighted at this news – and also somewhat relieved. He told me that Merton had received over three hundred applications for those three Senior Scholarships, and he had at times wondered if I would get one. He had been an undergraduate at Merton, before becoming a Fellow of the College, and he was sure I would find it a wonderful base for my research. He also mentioned that Jeremy Knowles had been a Senior Scholar at Merton in the late 1950s – something I did not know. I knew Radda kept in touch with Knowles, and was very touched when Knowles wrote to me a week later from Harvard, congratulating me on my scholarship, and offering a word of advice: 'Don't publish *too* much!'

Another success followed a few days later, when I received a letter from the European Molecular Biology Organization in Heidelberg, telling me that I had been awarded a Fellowship to work at the University of Utrecht in the Netherlands that summer. Radda had nominated me for the award, so that I could spend some time with colleagues in one of Utrecht's leading biophysical research groups, and learn from their approaches to some of the questions I was exploring. Even more commemorative bottles were added to the laboratory's shelves.

So I passed much of the long, hot and dry summer of 1976 in Utrecht, learning about new approaches to the biophysics of membranes, before returning to Oxford to move into Merton. The College provided me with a set of rooms in Holywell Street – a large study, bedroom and kitchen. As a student, I had never known such splendid accommodation. My rooms were now only five minutes' walk from the Department of Biochemistry, making it easy to work late in the evenings. However, I had no idea that my Senior Scholarship at Merton would finally and immediately allow me to achieve my heart's desire – to study theology *properly*.

IO

The Second Mountain: Theology

I settled into Merton quickly. I and the two other new Senior Scholars were under the benign supervision of Dr Michael Dunnill, who saw his role as ensuring that our time at Merton was as enjoyable and profitable as possible. He explained to me over lunch at the beginning of the new academic year that while Merton Senior Scholarships were now primarily awarded to support doctoral research, it had been the college's original intention that they could also be used to support a second first degree – in other words, to allow someone who already had (for example) an under-graduate degree in classics to supplement this with a second undergraduate degree in mathematics.

I realised immediately there might be a gateway here to studying theology. I went to my rooms and composed a cautious letter to Dunnill, asking him if we could explore the possibility of using my Senior Scholarship to continue my doctoral research under George Radda, while at the same time doing a second undergraduate degree in theology. I explained carefully that my doctoral research was at an advanced stage, due to some pieces of good fortune in Part Two of my chemistry degree. If the College agreed, I would complete my doctorate in molecular biophysics in my first year at Merton, while at the same time beginning study for Oxford's Final Honour School of Theology, and then devote myself totally to theology in my second and final year at the college. Oxford allowed students with 'advanced' status (in other words, those who had already completed a first degree) to take a second degree in two years, rather than three.

Dunnill asked me to come and talk this through with him in the middle of October, raising every conceivable objection to my proposed course of action. I was able to parry them all. 'This will have to go to Governing Body', he told me, referring to the weekly meeting of Fellows of the College, which made decisions about major issues of policy. 'It will be a fight, but I'll support you.' A week later, he asked me to come and see him again. My proposal would be discussed at the Governing Body on Wednesday, 3 November. He seemed much more hopeful about its prospects than before. 'You'll need to talk to George Radda. If he supports you, I think this will go through.'

I arranged to see Radda, and explained what I hoped to do, emphasising how much I had enjoyed working with him, and making it clear that my rapid progress in my research was largely his doing. Radda seemed to know what was coming. He and Jeremy Knowles were longstanding friends, and I wondered if Knowles might have said something to him about my theological aspirations. Radda made his position clear: it was essential that I completed my research and gained my doctorate. On the basis of my progress to date, I would have enough material for a good DPhil thesis by the end of that academic year. If I promised to make sure I completed my research by then, and submitted my thesis before the beginning of the following academic year, he would be delighted to support me. It was an easy promise to make, as that was exactly what I had intended to do.

I now had to wait impatiently and anxiously for the outcome of the Governing Body meeting. Dunnill wrote to me on Thursday, 4 November, telling me that his colleagues had agreed that I would be entered for the Final Honour School of Theology for examination in Trinity Term 1978, and that the College would meet the cost of my theological tutorials. He later filled in a little more detail of the Governing Body meeting, telling me that only one Fellow had raised any objection to the proposal, and that everyone else was on my side. Although it was now nearly half-way through Michaelmas Term, Merton's Senior Tutor suggested I should get started at once with my theology tutorials. Merton didn't admit undergraduates to study theology, so I would be looked after by Trevor Williams, chaplain of Trinity College, who would arrange for my teaching.

I met Williams at Trinity two days later. He was intrigued by what I proposed to do, and had already made some calls to line up tutors for me for the remainder of my first year studying theology. I could pack in eight initial tutorials on the New Testament in the remaining weeks of Michaelmas Term, assuming that I was happy to have two tutorials per week and continue into the vacation. Then I would have two or three sets of tutorials a week for the next four terms, after which I would start revising for the examinations in Trinity Term 1978. He asked if I was able to read Greek, which I would need for a compulsory New Testament translation paper. He was clearly relieved when I told him I was already reading the New Testament in Greek.

So a new and very demanding way of life began for me. I worked hard in the laboratory during the day, using the evenings and weekends to write the theological essays required for each tutorial in my rooms at Merton. It was easy to slip out of the laboratory discreetly from time to time for my tutorials in theology. Williams had arranged for me to be taught by some of Oxford's best scholars, as well as some rising stars: Robert Morgan (New Testament), John Barton (Old Testament), Paul Fiddes (systematic theology) and Andrew Louth (early Christian thought).

The Oxford tutorial system, which began to take shape in the nineteenth century, is one of the finest teaching tools ever devised. For each paper I was taking, I would be presented with eight essay titles, and a list of essential and optional reading. After reading through the material, I would then assemble my views on the topic in question, presenting and defending my conclusions in the light of the authors I had read. Having listened to me read my paper, my tutor would then discuss the topic for the remainder of the hour, filling in gaps in my understanding, and correcting any misreadings on my part. Without this intensive personal engagement, I do not think I could have mastered the material or the ideas. It was pure intellectual delight, as I began to grasp things that had eluded me, and saw connections I had never made before.

My anxieties about studying theology were dispelled within weeks. My first set of eight tutorials on the New Testament with Robert Morgan were sheer joy. Those tutorials began half-way through Michaelmas Term 1976 at Morgan's office in Wellington Square, and continued into the Christmas vacation over lunch at his home, followed by an extended walk through Wytham Woods, discussing the merits of Rudolf Bultmann's approach to the New Testament.

While studying theology was delightful, I nevertheless found it very demanding and challenging. The difficulty did not lie in the need to produce two essays (typically 2,500 words long) each week for my tutorials; I had become very good at summarising other people's arguments and assessing their internal coherence and evidential basis through my scientific research. What I lacked was a survey of the field – an explorer's sketch map of the theological landscape, which would help me locate thinkers and ideas, and work out how everything fitted together.

I found myself frustrated by the absence of a good introductory textbook comparable to the superb volumes I was used to in chemistry. What was the theological equivalent of March's *Advanced Organic Chemistry*? Or Cotton and Wilkinson's *Advanced Inorganic Chemistry*? One of the reasons that chemistry was such a satisfying academic subject to study was the quality of the introductions to the field, all written by experienced practitioners. I found no theological equivalent, and had to learn everything by myself. One day, I vowed to myself, I might try to write such an introductory textbook, aimed at people like me who had no previous knowledge of the field.

There were other challenges. Theology seemed to work by a set of rules that nobody seemed able to articulate clearly. There was no agreement on what constituted 'theological method'.

I was used to an evidence-based approach to scientific reasoning, which involved identifying a problem that needed to be solved, developing experiments that might resolve it, and interpreting the results of these experiments. This approach could be applied reasonably well to historical questions – such as 'What did Augustine of Hippo mean by original sin?' I could set out what various scholars thought, and check this against the primary sources. It did not, however, work well with purely conceptual questions, such as 'Does God suffer?' Few theologians seemed to agree about the criteria to be used in assessing possible answers to this type of question.

As I wrestled with this difficulty, I began to see it in context. I was already familiar with the idea that research tools are adapted to the subjects they investigate. Werner Heisenberg, one of the leading quantum theorists I studied in detail in my first year at Oxford, insisted that we know reality as we see this through our research methods. Theology seemed to use multiple research tools – philosophical, historical and textual. So why should I be surprised that there would be divergences between theologians over how these tools were used, or the relative priority that was to be given to them? I began to see that individual theologians crafted their own distinct approaches to their topic, gathering their personal perceptions about how best to weave these methods together. I decided I would actively work out for myself how best to do theology, rather than passively endorse someone else's approach.

Throughout the academic year 1976–7, I led a double life, undertaking research in the Department of Biochemistry to ensure I fulfilled my promise to George Radda by completing my thesis by the end of that year, while at the same time writing two sets of essays a week for tutorials in theology. Chris Morgan and I produced two further articles during the year – one reporting an original piece of research, and the other offering reflections on some core issues of how biological membranes were to be understood in the light of our research.[1] I discovered how to use 'broken time' – short periods of about fifteen minutes – effectively, so that I could make the best use of the intensely compressed schedule that resulted from doing two things at once.

Merton offered me a new set of rooms for the academic year 1977–8, located in the front quadrangle of the College. The process of moving took only a day, but disrupted my thesis writing, as my ancient typewriter was damaged during the move, and had to be replaced. During that summer, I was able to write up my DPhil thesis, and secure Radda's permission to submit it for examination. I submitted the thesis at the beginning of October, marking the end of my phase as a research scientist. In December, I dressed up in subfusc for my DPhil viva in the Examination Schools, and passed without the need for any corrections. George Radda sent me a congratulatory letter, wishing me well for the future.

I had, by this time, given careful thought to what I should do at the end of my time at Merton. I had been encouraged by many of my friends and colleagues to explore the possibility of ordination in the Church of England, and find some way of bringing the academic and the pastoral together in my future ministry. Some, however, warned me against this, pointing out that the Church of England was showing signs of disengaging from serious public discussion of theological issues and their wider significance. I might, they suggested, become a frustrated academic struggling to cope with the administration of a large parish church, unable to find time to think and write.

I met to discuss this possibility with Kenneth Woollcombe, Bishop of Oxford, who himself had served in academic theological positions in Oxford and New York. Woollcombe was very sympathetic and supportive, and persuaded me that I would be able to find ways of combining academic research with a pastoral role. He offered himself as a putative role model for the kind of integration that he had in mind, arguing that this represented the best possible way of doing theology. Woollcombe explained how he had served as a curate in Grimsby, which allowed him to gain pastoral experience and settle in to the culture of the Church of England, after which he had served in positions that allowed him to minister to both the soul and the mind. Woollcombe strongly recommended that I should leave Oxford after completing my theology degree at Merton, and prepare for ministry at his old training institution – Westcott House, Cambridge. I had been in Oxford for too long and needed to broaden my horizons. I admitted he was right, and raised no objection: I knew nothing about Westcott House, but was perfectly prepared to take his advice.

Woollcombe then arranged for me to attend a 'selection conference' at which a group of senior clergy and educationalists, chosen by the Advisory Council for the Church's Ministry (ACCM), would decide whether I was suited for ordination, and make a recommendation to him for my future. I was pleased at this development, as I was genuinely uncertain about whether this was a right move, and valued external assessment and guidance. If this wasn't right, I could see other paths ahead, such as finding a way of reconnecting with academic medical research – with my parents' fading hopes in mind – and developing my theological interests further in my own time.

The selection conference was a pleasant occasion, lacking the rigorous and critical engagement I had come to associate with Oxford academic interviews, but helpfully exploring possible future directions for my life. I left having no idea what the selectors had made of me, but valuing our conversations over my future options. As it turned out, they felt I had a genuine vocation to serve in the Church of England, and recommended me for training to the Bishop of Oxford. I went to visit Westcott House, and was offered a place to study there, with effect from September 1978.

In October 1977, I resumed the study of theology at Merton, packing in two (and sometimes three) tutorials each week to ensure I covered the curriculum. It was very demanding, in part because I had made a possibly unwise decision about the examination papers I would sit the following summer. The Oxford theology curriculum required students to choose an optional paper from a list of topics. One of them was science and religion – an obvious (and fitting) choice, which would allow me to explore in more depth some of the questions about science and faith I had been wrestling with in recent years. My tutor in science and religion was Peter Bide, chaplain of Lady Margaret Hall. It didn't take me very long to work out that Bide was the priest who had married C.S. Lewis to Joy Gresham in an Oxford hospital in 1957. From that point onwards, Bide and I became friends, discussing Lewis as much as science and religion at our weekly meetings. They were supposed to last an hour, but we both enjoyed them so much they went way over time.

But the list of optional papers included another that looked really interesting – scholastic theology. This would allow me to study the ideas of writers such as Anselm of Canterbury, Thomas Aquinas, Bonaventure, Duns Scotus and William of Ockham – all of whom were referenced extensively in more recent discussions of theological questions. Oxford was rich in teaching resources in this field. Reluctant to pass up on this opportunity, I decided to ask Merton if I could study *two* optional papers.

The College, by then well used to my eccentricities, took this in their stride, and gave me permission. I was taught by a team of able Catholic scholars: Edward Yarnold (Jesuit), Fergus Kerr (Dominican) and Cassian Reel (Franciscan). They helped me realise I could build friendships across denominational divides, as well as enabling me to immerse myself in what proved to be an outstandingly interesting field of study. The popular image of scholastic theology is that of a pointless debate about how many angels could dance on a pinhead. This is, of course, a myth, in that this bizarre debate never happened. What I actually encountered was a penetrating and rich discussion about the nature of theological language, the complexity of the interpretation of the Bible, and the subtle interplay of divine grace and human responsibility.

And there were others who generously helped me in ways I did not deserve. N.T. (Tom) Wright was a Junior Research Fellow at Merton during my time there, and enthused my study of the Pauline letters. Cheslyn Jones, Principal of Pusey House, helped me grasp the deep structure of John's Gospel. Tim Gorringe, chaplain of Wadham College, helped me appreciate the intellectual coherence of Karl Barth's vision of 'theological science', especially his insistence on a sustained theological engagement with the past. It was an exhilarating intellectual experience.

Then my aspirations for the future were threatened by a thunderbolt from the blue. Someone in Oxford University's administrative offices belatedly noticed that I was 'overstanding for honours'. I could not be awarded a classified honours degree in theology, because I had been a student at Oxford for too long. I would have to be content with simply passing the degree. The Senior Tutor at Merton told me that the Examination Regulations were quite precise on this matter, and there was no way round them – unless, of course, the College were to make an appeal to the University's chief executive body, the Hebdomadal Council, chaired by the Vice-Chancellor, to exempt me from this requirement. After making some inquiries, he told me that, while this was a rare request to make, he was confident that he could make a persuasive case for me, which would have the full support of the College.

He was right. On 1 December 1977, the *University Gazette* published a special decree passed by the Council at its weekly meeting. Towards the end of a series of decisions relating to major matters of academic policy was a short notice of relevance to only one person – me.

> A.E. McGrath, Merton College, who matriculated in Michaelmas Term 1971, is permitted to enter as a candidate for Honours in the Final Honour School of Theology in Trinity Term 1978, notwithstanding the provisions of Ch. VI, Sect. 1.C, §1, cl. 3.

The problem was removed. In effect, the decree stated that while I was technically ineligible for Honours under the existing regulations, the University had decided that this would simply be ignored in my case.

Meanwhile, those who taught me theology at Oxford were raising questions about my plans for the future. Would I *really* be happy working in the Church of England? Surely I ought to be thinking of an academic career? Training for ministry at Westcott House for two years could be intellectually tedious; should I not combine this training with some serious academic research? I could see the force of the argument, and had privately identified this as a potential problem, but there seemed to be nothing that could be done about it. In any case, I saw myself as testing my priestly vocation, being genuinely uncertain as to whether this was the right way ahead, even though it seemed the right option to explore at this stage.

Just after Easter, however, a colleague told me that St John's College, Cambridge, wanted to make an appointment to their Naden Studentship in Divinity – a one-year research position established in the eighteenth century, awarded from time to time, which offered a small stipend, limited dining rights on High Table, and access to the University of Cambridge's rather splendid library resources. No interview would be required, but I would have to provide a writing sample. The Studentship could be combined with other positions or responsibilities. I had nothing to lose, so sent off an application, including an essay I had written on Duns Scotus' theory of knowledge. The Master of St John's College, the historian Professor Nicholas Mansergh, wrote to me in the middle of June, offering me the Studentship, on the condition that I gained a good Second Class honours degree in theology. I accepted the offer. Everyone spoke well of the College, and it would be good to have an academic base at Cambridge.

Finally, after weeks of intense revision, I donned subfusc once more, and joined sixty other theology students for the Final Examinations in Theology. After several weeks, the results were posted. I was one of half a dozen students to be awarded First Class honours by the examiners. I wrote to Mansergh at St John's immediately to let him know the result, and was unconditionally elected to the Naden Studentship by the College council. Two days later, I met one of the examiners, who congratulated me on my 'remarkable achievement'. I told him I was really pleased with my result. He looked at me with astonishment. 'So they haven't told you yet?' I was obviously baffled by this, so he explained that I would be awarded the Denyer and Johnson Prize for the best performance in the Final Honour School of Theology that year. It turned out to be a very generous prize, which I used immediately to buy a complete set of Karl Barth's *Church Dogmatics*.

Shortly afterwards, I received an invitation to have lunch with a senior editor at Oxford University Press. Oxford is a very small place, and gossip spreads rather quickly. The Press had heard about my 'interesting career to date', he explained over lunch, and had an equally interesting possibility to discuss with me. Richard Dawkins' *Selfish Gene* (1976) had generated a huge amount of interest. Would I like to write an assessment and response from a Christian perspective? After much thought, I wrote a polite note thanking my colleague for lunch, and explaining that I did not yet feel ready to write such a book. There were many others better qualified, in my view – such as the biologist and theologian Arthur Peacocke. It would just be a matter of time before someone else wrote a book-length theological response to Dawkins' ideas.

In September, I packed my belongings, and prepared to take a coach to leave for Cambridge. I had been a student at Oxford for seven years. Oxford had shaped my development as a thinker. As the bus passed through the centre of Oxford and crossed Magdalen Bridge on its way east, I wondered if I would ever return to what Matthew Arnold so famously dubbed 'the Dreaming Spires'. I had simply no idea what would happen next.

I I

Wandering: Searching for a Calling

It was good to leave Oxford and move to Cambridge – or so I kept telling myself, as the bus meandered slowly across England in September 1978, leaving behind the city and University which had become such an important, even defining, part of my life. I had visited Cambridge twice over the summer, once I knew that I would be able to continue serious academic study at St John's College. My initial inclination had been to begin a research project in the field of science and religion. I had visited Dr Arthur Peacocke, Dean of Clare College, Cambridge, to explore the possibility of working with him. However, my conversation with him left me somewhat disappointed, and I decided not to take this any further.

Talking with Peacocke made it clear to me that I would not be able to make any significant progress in thinking about the relation of science and faith unless I had first acquired a much more thorough grasp of Christian theology. I had only begun to climb the mountain of theology, and had discovered that this was much higher than I had expected. Thanks to Paul Fiddes' enthusiasm, I had read some works of two leading German theologians while at Oxford – Jürgen Moltmann and Wolfhart Pannenberg – and had been impressed by their deep knowledge of the theological tradition. Both, I discovered, had begun their careers by a detailed engagement with a specific episode in the history of theology. Moltmann had studied the thought of a

French Huguenot theologian of the seventeenth century; Pannenberg had focused on the work of the medieval writer Duns Scotus. So why not lay the foundations for my dialogue between science and theology by looking at an important historical episode in depth?

It was not difficult to identify a suitable case study: the development of the scientific ideas of Nicolas Copernicus, exploring how these related to wider sixteenth-century theological debates involving Martin Luther or John Calvin. I went back to Cambridge for a further discussion – this time with Gordon Rupp, who had recently retired as Dixie Professor of Ecclesiastical History at Cambridge, and was England's leading authority on Martin Luther at that time. Emmanuel College had allowed Rupp to remain in his college office for two years after his retirement. At our meeting at Emmanuel, Rupp persuaded me that I had conceived a pointless project. It would be much better to focus on some aspect of the theology of Martin Luther, and use this to develop my historical and analytical skills. I could cope with Latin and German; why not focus on the development of Luther's doctrine of justification, which required a lot of further scholarly attention? He would enjoy supervising such a project, and he was sure I would like it.

At first sight, Rupp's proposal had nothing to do with the relation of science and faith. However, I was beginning to realise that exploration of this interface might have to wait for some considerable time, as I was simply not sufficiently competent in theology to make any meaningful contribution to its discussion. The risk of superficiality – which Jeremy Knowles had pointed out a few years earlier using the image of becoming a restless intellectual fox – loomed large over my thinking. Even at that early stage, it dawned on me that the field of science and religion was compromised by a lack of serious theological competency on the part of some of its conversation partners. I had enjoyed the Oxford paper on scholastic theology, particularly the important questions it opened up concerning the theology of grace and justification – the whole question of how human beings were put in a right relationship with God. Rupp's proposal made sense, and might be fun.

As I discussed this proposal with Edward Yarnold and others at Oxford during the late summer of 1978, I began to see the possibility of a grand research project, which would serve to deepen my grasp of theology, even though it had no obvious relation to the field of science and religion. My plan was this: I would take up Gordon Rupp's suggestion, and work on the development of Luther's doctrine of justification, setting this in its intellectual context in the late Middle Ages. Having done this, I could then broaden the project out in two ways. First, I could explore the intellectual development of the doctrine of justification throughout Christian history. Second, I could research the wider question of the intellectual origins of the theology of the European Reformation in the late Middle Ages and Renaissance. Rupp was a superb guide to Luther, and got my research off to a splendid start.[1]

At the same time as beginning my major research project, I was also preparing for ministry in the Church of England at Westcott House at the suggestion (which was really an instruction) of Kenneth Woollcombe, Bishop of Oxford. Woollcombe had encouraged me to see him as a friend and mentor, as he and I clearly had similar ideas about the role of theology in the ministry of the Church. However, eighteen months after the devastating early death of his wife from cancer, Woollcombe unexpectedly resigned as Bishop of Oxford. His departure left me without a mentor within an institution whose rules and conventions I did not really understand. This was a problem, as I did not really feel entirely comfortable with what I experienced as I began to train for ministry in the Church of England.

My hesitations, it must be understood, did not relate to my sense of calling to minister, especially through preaching. They were more focused on what I shall call Anglican exclusivism – the idea which I regularly encountered in certain (though happily not all) Anglican circles that other Christian denominations were inferior to the Church of England. I had read too much C.S. Lewis to indulge in any form of denominationalist imperialism or tribalism.

Lewis' famous image in the opening pages of *Mere Christianity* pointed to a common consensual Christianity, while recognising that this could be enacted in a number of ways. For Lewis, this common shared faith (which Lewis, borrowing a phrase from the Puritan writer Richard Baxter, styled 'mere Christianity') was like a hall, leading into several rooms. We do not live in the hall, but in the rooms that lead from it, in which 'there are fires and chairs and meals'.[2] To be a Christian is to align yourself with a denomination; yet what really matters is the shared consensual vision underlying all Christian groups, not any specific implementation of that vision which we might find particularly attractive for cultural, historical or personal reasons.

I had benefited from the wisdom of many Anglican scholars and theologians at Oxford, and felt at home within the Church of England's broad intellectual and cultural tradition. I loved the theology-drenched poetry of John Donne, George Herbert and Thomas Traherne, and had great admiration for scholar-bishops such as Ian Ramsey, who moved from the Nolloth Professorship of the Philosophy of the Christian Religion at Oxford University in 1966 to become Bishop of Durham. I had also been baptised in the Church of Ireland, which was part of the Anglican Communion. However, I tended to see myself primarily as a *Christian*, rather than as a signed-up *Anglican*. I never had any sense that the Church of England was superior to other Christian denominations, despite its obvious strengths. It was, however, a Church within which I felt comfortable, in that I was able to align myself with the generous orthodoxy of its core theological convictions, and locate myself within its broad range of implementations of the Christian vision.

After two years of training, I was deemed ready to begin professional ministry in the Church of England. Ordinands – the term used to refer to those in training for ministry – usually returned to serve in the diocese which sponsored them. Although I knew and loved the city and University of Oxford, I had no connection with Woollcombe's successor as Bishop of Oxford, and saw little point in returning there. My wife-to-be (Joanna, whom I had met at Oxford), however, was working in Nottingham, the main city in the diocese of Southwell. It turned out that Southwell had miscalculated their allocation of training parishes, and had been unable to fill four of their places for curates. The parish of St Leonard, Wollaton, a suburb of Nottingham close to its University, urgently needed a curate. After a visit to this busy fourteenth-century church, and a discussion with its rector, it was agreed I would serve as a curate in Wollaton. Joanna and I were married in Merton College chapel in July. I was ordained by the Bishop of Southwell in St Mary's, Nottingham, in September 1980.

The ordination service was a splendid liturgical and ceremonial event, though somewhat dampened by a rambling sermon that seemed to drift aimlessly from one irrelevancy to another, rather like a slightly dazed butterfly flapping around a flowery meadow. If I overlooked the sermon – and I rather suspect most present had forgotten what it was all about within an hour – it was a splendid and encouraging occasion. Perhaps working for the Church of England might not be as frustrating as some of my Oxford friends had suggested.

That consoling thought stayed with me for the best part of a month. Then somewhat different concerns began to make their appearance, despite my best efforts to suppress them. The first major event I attended after my ordination was a conference that was intended to give the clergy of the diocese of Southwell access to some cutting-edge thinking to invigorate their ministries. I was excited by this idea, and found myself looking forward to it with considerable anticipation.

It was especially exciting to discover that some workshops would deal with meditation and contemplation. I had recently begun to discover and appreciate the major spiritual writers of the Christian tradition, such as the fourteenth-century writer Thomas à Kempis, and was becoming aware of how important their approaches to contemplation could be to my own spiritual development, as well as the life of the Church. It would be good to hear an expert speak on this theme. I decided to take notes, to make sure I missed none of the wisdom that was to be so liberally dispensed.

I do not think that anything quite prepared me for the disappointment that lay ahead. On arrival, we learned that a potentially useful and interesting additional workshop

had been arranged – how to use computers for parish administration. After we had perused the rather unpromising
line-up of conference speakers displayed in the registration
area, there was an unseemly stampede to sign up for this
particular session. However, it soon became clear that the
five places available for the workshop had been preassigned
to the bishops and senior diocesan figures.

The specialist session on meditation that I had been
eagerly anticipating got off to a decidedly dubious start.
The dozen or so of us present were all made to sit in a circle
around a low table, and after a few minutes of increasingly
awkward silence, the leader reached into a plastic bag by his
feet and produced a moss-covered brick. It was not an especially attractive brick, giving the appearance of having been
rescued from a derelict and decaying building. We were then
invited to spend some time contemplating the brick, and
sharing our insights.

We sat in a stunned and subdued silence for some
moments, hardly daring to look at each other. My estima-
tion of a curate in a neighbouring parish soared when he
ventured the opinion that it was a rather *sad* brick, in that
nobody seemed to love it very much. That turned out to be
the intellectual high point of our contemplation. There were
a few more awkward moments when people coughed or
cleared their throats in preparation for saying something –
before eventually thinking better of it. I found myself
looking at the second hand of a large clock on the wall
ahead of me, urging it to move faster, so that this exercise in
pointlessness could come to an end.

I do not wish to exaggerate the importance of this inci-
dent. Clergy will tell you that diocesan conferences are
notoriously unpredictable, and that occasionally nuggets of

pure gold turn up in the midst of much that is dull, derivative and dispiriting. Gold was definitely in short supply at that particular conference, however.

I learned much in Nottingham, mainly about my own weaknesses and failings on the one hand, and the intelligence and wisdom of the laity on the other. It was lay people who pointed out the problems with my sermons, mainly concerning their lack of clarity and apparent inability to relate to the problems of Christian living. I might have defended myself by telling my critics that this was how I was taught to preach at Westcott House, but I did not. I listened and learned from those whom I felt called to serve. I realised that their views about preaching made more sense than those I learned in Cambridge, and decided to make them my own. I learned to love the parish Bible studies, which I led, and see people grow in faith and confidence as they made connections between the biblical text and their lives. And I learned to cope with the stress of being left on my own to run a busy parish, when its rector became ill and was off work for some considerable time.

My time in Nottingham caused me to admire both clergy and congregations, whom I came to see as loving and compassionate people, doing their best to look after each other and cope with the pain and sufferings of life, as well as the demands of an institution which sometimes seemed to offer them remarkably little in return for their financial support. More seriously, I became aware of the growing disjunction between a church and its wider context. I could hardly fail to wonder what the future held for the Church of England, given the growing disconnection between the language and culture of a parish church and the increasingly secular culture around it. Like many others, I came to wonder if I had been prepared for ministry in a church that no longer existed.

I did not give up on my hopes of being a theologian; if anything, these were intensified by my experience in Nottingham, not because I wanted to disconnect myself from the life of the Church, but because I felt theology needed to be brought into contact with that life in order to enrich and inform it, enabling it to address and cope with the cultural shifts taking place around it. My time in Nottingham taught me that a purely academic theology was inconceivable; all the great theologians of the Church had been pastors and preachers, and I resolved to follow in their footsteps. The role of the preacher was to be someone who was immersed in the riches of the Christian faith, and be able to make connections with the specific situation of their congregation.

I began to think of the preacher as an interpreter – someone who knew both the Bible and the rich tradition of reflection on the biblical text, yet who was grounded in a community to which this wisdom needed to be imparted and applied. I took visiting members of my congregation with the greatest seriousness, faithfully cycling round the streets of Wollaton virtually every afternoon, not simply because this was an expression of affirmation and care, but because my conversations with parishioners helped me to understand what I ought to be preaching about on Sundays. What questions were people asking? What difficulties were they facing? I was like someone who inhabited two worlds – the rich Christian theological tradition, and the everyday world of my congregation – and sought to interpret one to the other. They were the 'two horizons' I attempted to bridge in my preaching.

I owe much to two people who nourished the life of the Christian mind within me at that time: Douglas Davies and Richard McKinney, both lecturers in theology at the University of Nottingham, and both with links to Wollaton church. They became lifelines of encouragement and discernment, helping me to craft my own sense of calling as a theologian. In April 1983, after the birth of our second child, I began to reflect on where I should go next. I had been appointed for a period of three years, and my term of service at St Leonard's, Wollaton, would come to an end in the summer of 1983. I believed strongly in the notion of vocation, which was such an important theme to writers such as Martin Luther and John Calvin. Whereas many medieval spiritual writers – such as Thomas à Kempis, who I admired in many ways – saw vocation in terms of leaving the world and entering a monastery or convent, Luther and Calvin saw believers as called to serve God in the world, in ways that were adapted to their gifts on the one hand, and the needs of the community on the other.

Yet while Calvin tended to see vocation in terms of finding a predetermined social role, my own reading of the New Testament suggested it was better seen as the *construction* of a role. I might end up working in a role that seemed to deliver part of what I felt I was meant to be doing; it was then up to me to find some way of expanding this role to allow me to achieve the remainder. I saw my task as finding a good base for my ministry, while being willing to explore how this could be judiciously and creatively enhanced by continuing academic scholarship.

Those thoughts, however, did not solve the question of what I would do next. Then I noticed an advertisement in the *Church Times*. Wycliffe Hall, Oxford, was looking for a tutor in Christian doctrine and ethics. I knew Wycliffe Hall from my Oxford days, having heard some superb biblical expositions from Peter Southwell, its Senior Tutor. Wycliffe was a theological college that had been founded in 1877 to provide theological education for Oxford graduates intending to serve as clergy in the Church of England, and was then noted for its high academic standards and concern to connect the Bible and ministry. I shared, and continue to share, that concern. Over the years, it had developed good working relations with the Faculty of Theology at Oxford University, even though Wycliffe was outside the University's formal structures. Could this be the right way ahead?

I applied for the position and later discovered that it was the first time that Wycliffe Hall had ever advertised an opening like this, having previously relied on their networks to suggest names for such appointments. I was invited down for an extended discussion of the position with the Principal, Geoffrey Shaw, and his staff team, in which my understanding of the purpose and place of theology featured prominently. I went back to Nottingham afterwards, excited at the thought of being able to learn how to teach theology, and make connections with the serious business of Christian preaching. I had no real experience of teaching theology, but took comfort from the maxim usually attributed to Seneca the Younger: *docendo discimus* – 'we learn by teaching'.

A day after my return to Nottingham, Geoffrey Shaw called me to invite me to join the teaching staff of Wycliffe Hall. There would be no time limit on the contract. So late in the summer of 1983, Joanna and I returned to Oxford, along with our two young children. It was like coming home.

12

Oxford: Finding a Calling

There were three new members of staff at Wycliffe Hall when the new academic year began in September 1983: myself, the New Testament scholar David Wenham and John Went, an experienced pastor who had been appointed as Vice-Principal. I was succeeding Vernon White, an able theologian who had moved to the University of Exeter. In an act of great kindness, White had given me his lecture notes for all the courses he had taught. I drew on these substantially in my first year, allowing me the space I needed to develop my own approach, which I would begin to use the following year.

I was initially appointed as a tutor in doctrine and ethics at Wycliffe. Oxford, however, was rich in teaching resources, and the arrival of David Atkinson – initially as librarian of Latimer House and then as chaplain of Corpus Christi College – enabled the College to make good use of his expertise in ethics. My position was redesignated as Tutor in Doctrine, allowing me to focus on developing an introductory lecture course on Christian theology for those preparing for ministry, and a more advanced tutorial course for Wycliffe's students who were preparing for Oxford University's Final Honour School of Theology. My own experience of the difficulties I encountered at first in studying theology at Oxford was helpful in crafting my approach to teaching the subject.

Although I was not employed by Oxford University, I was elected a member of the Faculty of Theology early in 1984, and was then able to open some of my lectures at Wycliffe to the wider University community. Geoffrey Shaw encouraged me to develop a lecture course on the theology of the Reformation, which attracted students from beyond Wycliffe, and became a core component of the Faculty of Theology's teaching provision in this subject. As a result of my growing body of publications in this area, I was asked to consider several university positions in this field in the late 1980s and early 1990s, including the Directorship of the Institute for Reformation History at the University of Geneva. Although I considered some of these possibilities, it became clear to me that Wycliffe offered me everything I wanted at this stage in my life.

Why was Wycliffe such a satisfying place to work at this time? Under Geoffrey Shaw, it was a happy place, with a strong commitment to academic excellence on the one hand, and pastoral engagement on the other. I came to take this for granted; yet conversations with friends in comparable contexts suggested that this was actually relatively rare. I was working with colleagues whom I respected, while being encouraged to develop working links with the wider Oxford academic community. I was able to exercise a preaching and pastoral ministry within the college. And perhaps most important, I had excellent and highly motivated students, many of whom clearly had significant ministries ahead of them. Shaw was succeeded in 1989 by R.T. (Dick) France, a gentle, caring and perceptive pastor and teacher who was widely admired as a fine New Testament scholar. France led the college with patience and distinction through a difficult period in its history.

Most of Wycliffe's students were preparing for ordination in the Church of England, and wanted to immerse themselves in the study of theology so that it could inform their preaching. Perhaps because they had strongly pastoral inclinations, they offered me both encouragement and helpful feedback as I taught them in my first two years. It became clear to me very quickly that I would need to change my teaching in several ways, including making more explicit links between theology and preaching, perhaps showing how a given theological insight could be explained and applied. My students also suggested that I had assumed too much prior knowledge about theology on the part of my audiences; I would have to begin further back, and introduce material that I had thought they would already know. I tried to rise to these challenges, acknowledging that the students were right.

In 1985, I was asked to give a short series of lectures to the diocese of Oxford's part-time ministry course on Christology – the Christian understanding of the identity and significance of Jesus Christ. One of my lectures explored how a good understanding of Christology could function as the basis of preaching, and I mapped out a number of possibilities that I suggested had some promise. Two days later, I received a handwritten letter from Michael Green, who was then Rector of St Aldate's, one of the largest churches in Oxford. Green explained that he had never met me, but that he had been among the crowd listening to that particular lecture, and that the audience was 'buzzing' afterwards with enthusiasm. I had communicated some important points effectively, engagingly and accessibly. Might he encourage me, he asked, to keep speaking and start writing in this vein?

Green's affirming letter marked the beginning of our friendship, which continued until his death in 2019. He changed the way I understood myself. Up to this point, I had never considered myself to be anything other than an academic writer, trying to serve both the Church and the Academy through rigorous scholarship. Green's letter made me aware of the importance of writing accessibly and faithfully for a wider readership – and encouraged me to develop this skill. It was an art that Green himself had mastered, and he was more than willing to help me do the same. I published my first book written for a non-academic audience in 1986, and this continues to be an important aspect of my writing and speaking ministry to this day.

By 1990, I had developed what I felt was a workable course in the basics of Christian theology, which served as a genuine introduction to the field, assuming virtually no previous knowledge. My sixteen lectures at Wycliffe Hall were well attended and attracted the notice of Blackwell Publishers, an Oxford-based academic publishing company, who asked if they could discuss publishing this lecture course in a suitably revised form. When I expressed interest in the possibility, they asked some prominent theologians in the United States and the United Kingdom to make suggestions about what approach I should adopt. Unfortunately, each provided radically divergent answers, none of which was pedagogically viable.

In the end, the publishers and I reached an amicable agreement. The views of the 'experts' would be set to one side. I would write an introduction to *Christian* theology, not any specific *form* of Christian theology. The work would include discussion of Protestant, Catholic, Orthodox and Evangelical approaches to theology, treating all with respect and ensuring they were properly represented; but it would not commend or adopt any of these specific views. It would be descriptive not prescriptive, allowing its users to understand what had been thought rather than telling them what to think. It would let them make up their own minds on core theological questions, rather than direct them to predetermined conclusions. And above all, it would assume that its users had virtually no prior knowledge of Christian theology. Everything would be introduced and explained. We agreed that the length of the work would be appropriate to this level of explanation, and I was free to determine what this might be.

So I happily set to work, using the core lectures of my Oxford theology course as the basis of the book's sixteen chapters. Everything was reworked to ensure consistency of style and level. The text was written in simple English prose, avoiding any colloquial expressions or turns of phrase that readers with English as their second language might find difficult. I gave careful thought to what issues would be covered and how they would be explained, checking these out on my student audiences, and inviting students to read and assess draft sections of the work. The process of revision may have been slow and painstaking, but it ensured the work could be understood without the need for external help. Each chapter would include some study questions to allow users to check out whether they had understood its contents.

Blackwell Publishers had hoped that the book would be about two hundred pages long; it turned out to be nearly three times that length. It was the theology textbook I had hoped for when I began to study the subject back in 1976. But because it covered so much ground, and offered so much help to its readers, it was *long*. So would there be a market for such a potentially expensive book? There was only one way to find out.

The textbook was published with the unimaginative (but accurate) title *Christian Theology: An Introduction* in 1993, offering itself as a genuine introduction to Christian theology, aimed especially at those who were new to the field. The book quickly became Blackwell's bestselling book, and set new standards of clarity of presentation and reliability of explanation in the field. Translations followed into fifteen languages, although many European seminaries and universities adopted the English text of the work because it was so easy to read in comparison with the German textbooks they had hitherto used. We received extensive feedback from academics who adopted it, and made numerous corrections, additions and revisions in the second edition, published three years later. Its critical and commercial success led me to write several further textbooks in the field. Today, the work is in its sixth edition, and continues to be one of the world's most widely used theological textbooks.

In 1995, following Dick France's decision to return to parish ministry in the Church of England, I became Principal of Wycliffe Hall, and focused my attention on how best to prepare men and women for ordination, and equip them theologically in order to encourage and resource the churches as they faced increasing challenges about their social role and the intellectual coherence of their foundational ideas. My first action was to strengthen the relation of Wycliffe Hall to the University of Oxford by initiating the process by which it was recognised as a Permanent Private Hall of the University, allowing its students more access to the University's resources, as well as enabling Wycliffe to benefit from the institutional wisdom of other colleges.

Although my contract made no reference to the length of my term of office, I considered it to be a ten-year position. My conversations with others who had held similar senior positions suggested that burn-out was the inevitable outcome of a longer period of service. Geoffrey Shaw had lasted ten years before retiring, and Dick France six. I continued to teach a core course in Christian theology, seeing this as an integral aspect of preparing people for positions of leadership in the churches and resourcing their preaching.

As my publication record expanded, I began to receive invitations to put my name forward for professorships of theology in leading universities and seminaries in North America. I was quite clear that my future lay in serving in the United Kingdom, but did not wish to cause offence to my American and Canadian colleagues. As a result, I found myself inventing reasons for declining to discuss these positions. I was thus relieved when Oxford University awarded me the *ad hominem* title of 'Professor of Historical Theology' in 1999 as a formal recognition of my international reputation in my field of study. I would enjoy all the privileges of an Oxford professorship – except, of course, a salary.

This personal chair in theology gave me an excellent (and genuine) excuse to resist enticements to leave the United Kingdom. I wanted to stay in Oxford, and serve both the Academy and Church. Moreover, I also saw this award as a landmark, a recognition by my peers at Oxford and beyond that I had climbed my theological mountain. It would now be possible for me to begin to explore the relationship between science and Christian theology in an intelligent and informed way, having secured my credibility in both areas of research. I finally felt that the critical issue Jeremy Knowles had raised twenty-five years earlier had been resolved.

Meanwhile, work continued at Oxford – running a college, lecturing in theology, supervising graduate students, publishing and developing Wycliffe's profile through public speaking engagements. For example, in 2000 the Archbishops of Canterbury and York invited me to deliver the opening sermon for the General Synod of the Church of England in Westminster Abbey in the presence of Queen Elizabeth II. I spoke about the need to affirm and welcome cultural engagement without passively accepting the cultural fashions of the day.[1]

By 2000, I had come to appreciate the importance of apologetics – the enterprise of engaging wider cultural concerns and questions about religious belief, displaying the intelligibility of Christianity and its capacity to engage the realities of human experience, raising questions about its cultural alternatives, and translating the vocabulary of the Christian faith into terms that could connect up meaningfully with a secular culture. I became involved in some local Oxford discussions around this time about the rationality of faith, including taking part in a three-way private debate on this matter in Balliol College with two prominent Oxford atheist scientists: Peter Atkins and Richard Dawkins. I was no prophet, but could see that their form of scientific atheism would become a major challenge to Christianity in the next decade.

My mind went back to my lunchtime conversation in the summer of 1978 with a senior editor from Oxford University Press, who had urged me to write a theological response to Dawkins' *Selfish Gene*. I had declined because it seemed obvious that there were others who were better placed than I was to write this. Yet to my surprise, nobody had taken up this challenge. In the meantime, I had read everything

Dawkins wrote, and mapped out how I might respond to the questions he raised.

In 2003, twenty-five years after the possibility was first raised, I decided that, since nobody else had published a theological analysis and assessment of Dawkins' views about science and religion, I would do this myself, in preparation for what I now believed to be an inevitable showdown. *Dawkins' God* was published in 2004, mapping out some of his criticisms of faith and developing responses to those concerns.[2] Naturally, I also raised questions about Dawkins' own approach, which seemed to represent an uncritical scientific positivism married to a populist cultural distaste for religion. Perhaps because of its incubation period of a quarter of a century, the work was unusually coherent and focused, and was correspondingly well received.

I also introduced a course on the basics of apologetics at Wycliffe Hall, which I later taught alongside Michael Green, fighting hard to ensure this became an integral aspect of theological education in the Church of England. But I failed utterly, for reasons that continue to puzzle me. I found myself isolated on this issue – not within the Oxford intellectual community, which welcomed such discussions about the interface of theology and culture, but within the Church of England, which saw them as peripheral and distracting. The bureaucrats of the Church of England seemed to think that teaching students about issues of Anglican polity was more significant than ensuring the survival of Christianity as a serious option for thinking people in Western culture.

It would be an exaggeration to say that I faced a crisis in 2004; it was more that I was confronted with a probable parting of the ways that I hoped would never happen. I was fully committed to the theological education of the clergy and laity of the churches, including enabling them to deal with the cultural challenges that I was sure lay around the corner – just as I was firmly persuaded of the importance of serious scholarship and its capacity, when rightly applied, to enrich the ministry of the Church. The ability and willingness of the Church of England to hold these together and value them both had been one of its greatest strengths in the past. However, this synthesis now seemed to be unravelling. Richard Harries, Bishop of Oxford at that time, was clearly capable of this kind of public engagement; yet he sometimes seemed to be a lonely voice in the face of a growing tendency within the Church of England to believe that reaching out required dumbing down.

Perhaps I misread the situation, but I sensed that the Church of England was losing its capacity to engage with major cultural issues in an intellectually serious way, and was developing policies for the training of its clergy that could only make things worse. This was certainly a concern that emerged from my reading of the Church of England's 2003 report *Formation for Ministry within a Learning Church* (often simply known as 'the Hind Report'). This unsatisfactory document created competition between the Church of England's theological colleges, which had up to that time worked together collegially. It proposed well-meaning changes to teaching and training practices that would, in effect though not in intention, inevitably lead to a reduction in the quality of the education of clergy. In the 1980s, ordinands generally had a strong inherited knowledge of the Christian tradition, which theological education was able to *enhance*. Yet it was clear that shifts were taking place within British Christianity that meant that theological education now had to *establish* that knowledge in the first place – and what the Hind Report proposed would not allow theology to be taught in sufficient depth or detail to sustain the teaching and preaching ministries of future clergy.

I began to feel that I was in the wrong place, and that I needed to find a new role. In 2004, after nine years as Principal of Wycliffe Hall, I resigned in order to establish the Oxford Centre for Christian Apologetics and serve as its first Director. Once this fledgling institute settled down, I could step back and play a lesser role, allowing me to think about what I would do next. Happily, the new Centre quickly established itself. I could move on to something new. But what?

13

The Two Peaks: The View from the Top

Finding your calling often involves identifying your own gifts, and considering how these relate to what needs to be done. My own journey of faith had convinced me of the importance of gaining a proper understanding of the Christian faith at both the personal and communal level, and helping others to grow in their faith and understanding. I had been able to do this at Wycliffe Hall by helping future clergy to work out how to teach and preach Christian theology, while developing my senior academic role as Oxford University's Professor of Historical Theology.

It was now clear that I would need to reinvent myself, in order to find a new role that would allow me to minister within the Church of England, be involved in the theological education of its clergy, and retain a senior academic research and teaching role at Oxford or another world-class university. I had long wanted to explore the complex and contested area of 'natural theology', seeing this as offering both an interface between theology and the natural sciences, and an intellectual platform for engaging with wider cultural issues. This would allow me to mingle theology and apologetics.

Happily, the John Templeton Foundation agreed that this was an important topic, and offered to fund a Senior Research Fellowship for me at Harris Manchester College, Oxford, for two years from September 2006, so that I could focus on this theme and prepare myself for the future. Under its visionary Principal, Ralph Waller, this College had established a strong profile in the field of science and religion, making it an ideal base for my research. This Fellowship would give me time to reflect on my future, in that it had no administrative responsibilities of any kind, allowing me to focus entirely on some key research and writing projects.

I had not given any major endowed lectures series since I delivered the Bampton Lectures at Oxford in 1990,[1] given the pressure on my time. Once colleagues became aware that I had secured a position that allowed me ample opportunity for research and writing, I was invited in quick succession to give the Riddell Memorial Lectures at the University of Newcastle (2008), the Gifford Lectures at the University of Aberdeen (2009) and the Hulsean Lectures at the University of Cambridge (2009–10) – in each case, engaging the topic of natural theology. These invitations called for a significant investment of time in writing three sets of lectures, and then turning each into a major academic monograph. I was able to prepare much of the material during my time at Harris Manchester College.

My decision to return to the academic world was validated in the most striking manner during my first month as a Senior Research Fellow at Oxford. Richard Dawkins' atheist manifesto *The God Delusion* was published in the summer of 2006, and became an international bestseller. Dawkins declared himself to be at war with a vague generality he designated 'religion', with science as his weapon of choice. His haughty and condescending oracular tone, along with some less than subtle hints that agreeing with him placed you on the right side of history, ensured that Dawkins' book would have a substantial public impact. A response was obviously needed – quickly. I realised I could do this. The very positive reception of *Dawkins' God* (2004) had created a public perception that I knew more about Dawkins' views on science and religion than anyone else. I had read *The God Delusion* in preparation for a debate with Dawkins on BBC television a few weeks earlier. And my new academic role allowed me the time I would need to write a response *immediately*, without needing to consult or gain permission from anyone.

In September 2006 I wrote to the London-based Christian publisher SPCK, offering to produce a 25,000-word response to Dawkins within six weeks, on condition that they fast-tracked it, so that it would be published in January or February 2007. SPCK agreed enthusiastically, and a contract was drawn up and signed within a week. I collaborated with Joanna, who as a psychologist was able to deal with some of Dawkins' interesting though somewhat superficial and misguided digressions in that field. Our response was published as *The Dawkins Delusion? Atheist Fundamentalism and the Denial of the Divine*. It became an international bestseller.

Other more considered and detailed critiques of Dawkins would subsequently appear from other writers, adding a welcome depth and range to the debate.[2] *The Dawkins Delusion?* was, however, the first significant Christian engagement with Dawkins to be published, and shaped the direction of the subsequent discussion. I could never have written that book without the flexibility and status of my academic role, and the freedom of expression that this allowed me.

Since then, the New Atheism has predictably become a victim of its own boom and bust cycle, and has lost its initial social traction. It is now seen as an incorrigibly modern movement, dominated by ageing, white, middle-class,

Western men, which is intensely vulnerable to postmodern suspicions about claims to universality and objectivity, failing to acknowledge (precisely because it fails to *recognise*) that it is itself shaped by cultural influences and assumptions. The widespread rejection of the narrow and rigid Enlightenment view of human rationality within academic and progressive cultural circles in recent years has left the New Atheism stranded on a rationalist sandbank, while everyone else is busy exploring other, equally rational, ways of understanding and engaging with our world.

My own view is that the New Atheism represented a naive scientific positivism unsullied by any serious engagement with the history or philosophy of science. It gained cultural attention largely through its crude parody of religion which baffled religious believers while resonating with the anti-religious prejudice and ignorance that was then becoming endemic within Western culture. Reading Dawkins' arguments for atheism in 2006 made me a little nostalgic, in that they were so similar to mine back in 1970, before I was awoken from my dogmatic slumbers by reading Karl Popper, who served as a gateway to a historically and philosophically informed approach to the natural sciences.

I now found myself being treated as a public intellectual by the media, being rolled out predictably for what were often highly superficial debates about religious issues, particularly in relation to science. It was not a role that I found intellectually satisfying, mainly because of the media's constant demand for *simple* answers which did not fit easily with the complexities disclosed by serious historical research. Popularisation entails simplification which in turn risks distortion.[3] I felt I was in danger of becoming a traitor to the world of scholarship, particularly as this was not simply disregarded but was actively *devalued* in popular debates about science and faith. 'We don't want to hear this,' one producer told me. 'But you *need* to hear this,' I replied.

Perhaps because I was seen as able to engage the cultural issues facing the Church at that time, I was sounded out about senior leadership roles in the Church of England. I was invited to 10 Downing Street to discuss my future in the Church with the Prime Minister's appointments advisor, who took the view that I should see myself as a potential bishop or dean of a cathedral, and asked me to keep in touch with him as possibilities emerged over the next few years.

I very much appreciated the advisor's helpful perspectives on my situation, but felt he had overestimated my potential for such a role. My talents related primarily to the life of the mind. The days of scholar-bishops in the Church of England, such as Ian Ramsey, now seemed to me to lie in the past. I would be overwhelmed by the administrative load that now went with the positions of dean or bishop. Those roles required special gifts – gifts that I did not believe I possessed, even though some seemed to think otherwise. My hunch – and it was nothing more than a hunch at this stage – was that I ought to remain in the Academy, and find some way of serving congregations that would not be part of my job description, but would unquestionably be part of my calling.

In the autumn of 2007 I was approached by King's College London, to ask if I might be interested in applying for a new chair of theological education that it proposed to establish within its Department of Education and Professional Studies with effect from September 2008. King's College had been founded by King George IV and the

Duke of Wellington in 1829 to encourage a creative interaction between the Academy, Church and society, and had a
long tradition of fostering serious theological engagement
and reflection. There was no question of being *offered* this
position; King's College initially wanted to make sure that,
if they funded such a chair, there would be a good pool of
candidates. The proposed chair would require its occupant
to undertake theological research, teach graduate courses in
theology aimed primarily at clergy, and supervise research
students. I expressed interest. In the spring of 2008, I was
informed that the College had agreed to establish this
new chair, to be known as the Professorship of Theology,
Ministry and Education, and was now inviting applications
for the post. I applied, and was interviewed along with two
other senior academics, both of whom would have been
admirable choices for the position. Three hours later, I was
offered the job.

It was sad to leave Oxford, but I knew it was a good move.
King's College was a leading international research university. London would offer me an entirely new educational
and cultural experience. My new office was close to Waterloo
Station, and overlooked the south bank of the Thames, with
the Houses of Parliament to my left, St Paul's Cathedral to
the right, and the National Theatre straight ahead. So I
joined the stream of regular commuters from Oxfordshire
to central London, experiencing the frustrations of railway
travel in an age of overcrowding and underinvestment.

This academic role in the British metropolis allowed me
new opportunities to work with major London institutions
such as Westminster Abbey and St Paul's Cathedral in engaging with the great issues of our time from a theological
perspective. I was able to do some serious academic research,

while at the same time engage issues of theology and culture with graduate students. Many of these were clergy of the Church of England, trying to bring academic depth and integrity to their ministries. To my delight, I was also invited to teach an MA course in science and religion, which King's College had established in order to meet growing demand for serious academic input in this area. I did not, however, lose my links with Oxford. Harris Manchester College generously and unexpectedly extended my Senior Research Fellowship indefinitely, and provided me with a small office in the college so that I could work there when I was in Oxford.

My London chair allowed me to develop my career as a scholar, teach in the fields of both theology in general, and the specialist field of science and religion, and remain a resource to those ministering in British churches – including, but not limited to, the Church of England. On being appointed to King's College, I wrote to Downing Street, thanking them for their interest in me, but asking not to be considered for any senior position in the Church of England in the future, in that I no longer felt I would be able to accept such a position if it were to be offered to me. I remained firmly committed to serving the Church of England, however, in a more modest role, better adapted to my abilities. I met with my local Anglican bishop, and arranged to become part of a team of clergy in a group of rural parishes near our home in the Cotswolds, enjoying leading services and preaching to small yet engaging and intensely faithful country congregations.

Working in these country parishes helped me become bilingual theologically. I spoke about theology in one way to academic audiences, and another way when I was preaching to rural congregations. I had to learn the skill of translating my ideas into words, images and stories that would connect up with my audience. C.S. Lewis had always emphasised the importance of 'learning the language of your audience', and translating your ideas effectively yet reliably in different contexts.

Finally, in September 2013 I was asked to consider returning to Oxford as the Andreas Idreos Professor of Science and Religion, and Director of the Ian Ramsey Centre for Science and Religion, with a brief to deal with every aspect of the relation of science and religious faith, both in terms of the history of this relationship and its contemporary forms. It was the job I had longed for, allowing – indeed *demanding* – that I explore the relation of science and religion in depth and detail, especially in the light of contemporary academic discussions and public debate.

Following a preliminary discussion with the Chair of Oxford's Faculty of Theology and Religion to clarify some matters, I allowed my name to go forward. After an interview in November, I was offered the position, and began my new role at Oxford in April 2014. For the first time in my life, I was employed by Oxford University – or, to use the proper form of words going back to the Middle Ages, by 'the Chancellor, Masters and Scholars of the University of Oxford'. As it happened, the Idreos chair was attached to a Professorial Fellowship at Harris Manchester College, allowing me to remain associated with this very special Oxford community of students and scholars. Needless to say, I continue to serve as part of a clergy team in Cotswold parishes to this day.

No job is perfect, and I soon found that I missed lecturing to London metropolitan audiences, which often included senior academics, financiers, politicians, diplomats and civil servants. The question times after these lectures were highly stimulating, and there was no real equivalent to these audiences in Oxford. Colleagues therefore suggested that I should apply for the Gresham Professorship of Divinity, a three-year appointment that fell vacant in September 2015. This was the oldest and most distinguished chair of public theological engagement in Britain, having been established in 1597 with the foundation of Gresham College in the City of London. I would be required to give six public lectures in divinity each year in the City of London over a period of three years. The audiences I could expect were those I had found so rewarding in the past.

I needed Oxford University's permission to allow my name to be considered for this position. After due consultation, I was both permitted and encouraged to put my name forward. My two distinguished predecessors in this role had lectured on religion and the arts, and religion and politics respectively. My suggestion that I lecture on religion and the natural sciences was warmly received by Gresham College, and was clearly a good choice. The large audiences these lectures attracted necessitated a move to a more spacious public venue in the City of London. Gresham College kindly offered to extend my contract by a year, although I was by then so busy with additional responsibilities in Oxford that I was unable to take up this generous offer.

Looking back, I now see holding the Oxford Idreos Professorship in Science and Religion as the culmination of my journey of discovery that I mapped out on the deck of a ferry crossing the Irish Sea on a winter night in December 1971. Yet I could never have predicted that the journey would take this particular form. Perhaps that is true of all our thinking about the nature of our vocation. We are provided with a compass that gives us bearings, rather than a detailed map that defines our destination. I had learned to be content with seeing through a glass darkly, being unable to see clearly where I was heading or what I was meant to be doing, but somehow finding my way to roles that seemed to fit. Sometimes our lives make more sense when we look backwards, and see a pattern emerge where we had once thought there was none.

I had climbed two mountains – science and theology – allowing me to survey the rich and complex view from the top of these twin peaks, and tell others of what I could now see. I found new answers to old questions, observing them from fresh perspectives and in a new light – a topic I shall explore in the next part of this work, as I revisit some of the issues that I had once thought I had resolved decisively, but now turned out to be rather more complicated than I had originally perceived, and demanded the creation of new vistas of understanding and insight.

PART THREE

Old Questions, New Insights:
Living on the Island of Faith

14

On Reconsidering What Once Seemed Obvious

In February 2018, I was invited to write an imagined letter to myself as a teenager.[1] It was a worthwhile but troubling experiment in which I, a hardened and critical old man, wrote to a naive and idealistic boy who had no idea what would happen to him during the intervening fifty years.

I knew very well what I thought back in the late 1960s, and could see how so many of my seemingly secure and robust beliefs would crumble and collapse over the next half-century, cruelly exposed as inadequate. My free-thinking may have been unconstrained by any external authority; it nevertheless led me to a place that proved to be intellectually uninhabitable. Here is how that short letter began:

> I know things seem simple and obvious to you. You think all the big questions of life can be settled by science. You think that believing in God is outdated and irrational and that you should only believe things that can be proved. I don't think you are ready to hear this yet, but things just aren't that simple.

It was a fair point, even if I made it somewhat condescendingly in that imagined letter. History unkindly exposes so much of what one generation regarded as settled certainties to be little more than the transient conventional wisdom of the day. The philosopher Alfred North Whitehead criticised such trends in the period of soul-searching that followed the catastrophe of the First World War: 'Should we not mistrust the jaunty assurance with which each generation believes it has at last got the concepts with which to make sense of the world?'[2]

Looking back on the 1960s, I can see Whitehead's words came closer to expressing a universal truth than some of the more ambitious philosophies of that restless age. Taking a cue from the ancient Greek philosopher Heraclitus of Ephesus, we have to come to terms with being caught up in a ceaselessly changing world, in which what once seemed to be certainties are swept away by the passing of time. Many of the views that were regarded as enlightened and modern in the 1960s are now seen as located in (perhaps even created by) a specific historical and cultural context that lies firmly in a vanished world.

I make no criticism of my former self in holding such views. I can, however, now see a persistent pattern in my teenage years – a general intolerance of uncertainty, and a reluctance to recognise the complexity of life's biggest questions. I wanted to be on the right side of history, and aligned myself with ideas and groups that were seen as 'progressive'. I was young, prone to being an intellectual chameleon who absorbed the culturally acceptable views of my day without any critical interrogation. What I thought was 'freethinking' turned out to be thinking along somewhat rigid lines predetermined by self-styled progressives. It was not until the spring of 1971 that I really began to think freely and for myself, having been awoken and energised by Karl Popper and others.

I now realise that many beliefs that I considered to be facts in the late 1960s were really little more than 'intellectual fashions' and 'transitory values of the day',[3] whose (fleeting) popularity was unwisely taken as an indication of their reliability. I have come to understand that our world is much more complex and that our intellectual vision is less penetrating and perceptive than I had once believed. We see through a glass darkly, not with the crystalline clarity that my early scientific rationalism had promised.

Many mistakenly hope to find an island of certainty as they journey over the sea of life, offering clear answers to their deepest questions. But history suggests that each such island offers only the semblance of certainty and a tenuous link with the world of experience. The Comtean Positivism of the nineteenth century, the Logical Positivism of the twentieth century, and the New Atheism of the early twenty-first century are all fallen idols that failed to deliver the secure knowledge that they promised. The New Atheism may have aspired to rid us of our delusions; it has ended up being numbered among them. We have to come to terms with uncertainty without being overwhelmed by it.

Earlier in this work I described the process of unravelling and disintegration of what seemed to me to be the iron-clad certainties of reason and science. What I had assumed to be unassailable and self-evidently true was exposed as provisional and fallible; a worldview that I considered unsinkable foundered on the iceberg of historical scholarship and rigorous philosophical criticism. Having been shipwrecked on an island, I naturally tried to salvage what I could from this wreckage, finding some things that could indeed be retained and put to new use.

So where do I stand now? I was once shipwrecked on a strange island of faith; I have now become its long-time resident, taking pleasure in showing new arrivals around its landmarks, and recounting the story of my own discovery of this place of refuge. How as an older man do my views about science, faith and the quest for reliable knowledge relate to those I held as a teenager? In this final section I shall explore what I have learned on these matters, beginning by reflecting more critically on what happened during my first term at Oxford University, as I moved decisively from atheism to Christianity.

15

Seeing Reality:
Christianity as a 'Big Picture'

In my first term at Oxford University I was drawn to Christianity primarily because of the quality of its vision of reality. It was like a lens that seemed able to bring clarity to what the Harvard psychologist William James described as the 'great blooming, buzzing confusion' of reality,[1] enabling me to appreciate its fundamental unity, while at the same time affirming the distinctiveness of its individual elements and aspects. I discovered that Christianity possessed a rare and refreshing ability to hold these multiple facets together in a coherent whole, while at the same time preserving their distinct identities. I began to appreciate the wisdom of the Cambridge physicist Alexander Wood: 'This is our first demand of religion – that it should illumine life and make it a whole.'[2]

As this narrative makes clear, I had been reflecting over a period of several years during the late 1960s on a range of issues relating to the meaning of life, the scope of the scientific method, and the intellectual credentials of atheism. I went through an extended period of intellectual incubation at Methody, in which I endlessly scrutinised the great questions of science and faith without securing their resolution. My mind was full of disconnected ideas and partial insights, focusing on what was little more than a growing hunch that Christianity had some traction on a deeper reality that I had yet to encounter or discover. Then, in Michaelmas Term

1971, everything fell into place in an imaginative synthesis: a shadowy intellectual landscape was unexpectedly illuminated in a fleeting moment of breathtaking lucidity and depth of vision, leaving me with the memory of an instant of stunning clarity, and a longing to recapture its detail. I felt some sympathy for the novelist Virginia Woolf, who wrote of her exasperation at sensing tantalisingly brief moments of insight in which she perceived 'some real thing behind appearances',[3] only to find that she was totally unable to prolong the experience or pin it down.

Yet although I could *see* how the Christian faith held things together, I was frustratingly unable to express this in words. Dante seemed to describe much the same dilemma in the final canto of his *Divine Comedy*, noting that Christianity provides a vision of a transcendent reality that proves tantalisingly resistant to verbal expression:

> From that moment onwards my power of sight exceeded
> That of speech, which fails at such a vision.[4]

To this day, I struggle to explain exactly what catalysed my imaginative epiphany. Whatever its cause may have been, though, I experienced a sudden crystallisation of clarity within my mind, which changed everything. I *knew* – I could *see* – that things could be held together within a Christian framework.

In one sense, my conversion to Christianity was cerebral and intellectual, reflecting my awareness of its capacity to make sense of a complex world. Yet one critical point in that intellectual journey was *imaginative*, as I saw how things could be held together in a moment of insight that melded my rational ideas into a coherent whole (I believe John

Ruskin meant something like this when he spoke of a 'penetrative imagination'). My moment of insight and illumination allowed me to see that things *could* be held together coherently, while leaving me to work through the details of *how* this might be done.

As I reflected on this, I realised that a similar pattern of imaginative discovery could be seen in the history of the natural sciences. Back in the early 1970s, the philosophy of science was still dominated by rationalist theories of scientific reasoning and discovery, such as Carl Hempel's Deductive-Nomological Model, but the tide was now shifting towards a recognition of the role of the imagination in theory development.

In 1963, the Nobel laureate Sir Peter Medawar – widely regarded as one of the most influential British public intellectuals of his day – published an article in *The Times Literary Supplement* arguing that an imaginative or inspirational process is an integral element of scientific reasoning.[5] Scientists should not feel inhibited in speaking about creativity or the role of the creative imagination in theory development. A rational discovery could be made by imaginative means. These ideas are now mainstream within the philosophy of science, which has moved away from the rigid rationalism of an early period and recognised the complexity of the process of scientific discovery.[6]

While I was relieved to know that my own road of discovery was neither irrational nor unscientific, I soon learned that it was not in any way representative. Most students described their conversion experiences in terms of a joyful release from guilt, a discovery of their personal significance and value in the sight of God, or the forging of a secure personal relationship with Christ. I could understand all of these, and considered them to be affirmed by my own emerging way of thinking. But I had yet to find an intellectual soul-mate who shared my journey to faith through the evangelical illumination of a shadowy landscape of reality. Many came to appreciate this after their conversion; nobody that I knew, however, had found it to be the *cause* of their conversion.

William James came close to my own view in suggesting that religious faith was fundamentally 'faith in the existence of an unseen order of some kind in which the riddles of the natural order may be found and explained'.[7] James' notion of an 'unseen order' expressed the idea of constructing or discerning some intellectual framework or mental map that would disclose the interrelatedness of things. It seemed to me that Christianity was able to 'colligate' – to borrow a term from the empirical philosopher William Whewell, meaning 'to hold or knit together'– our experiences and observations, locating them within a grander picture of reality. I had not yet, however, encountered anyone who framed Christianity as I did. Was I completely on my own, or would I eventually find someone else who took a similar approach?

In February 1974, I began to read the works of C.S. Lewis, and found myself overwhelmed by his essay 'Is Theology Poetry?' This remarkable piece set out his view of Christianity's imaginative capacities, which both acknowledged and enfolded the messy diversity of the world, allowing it to be seen as a coherent but not homogenous whole. Lewis, admittedly, seems to have borrowed this idea of a 'big picture' from Dante,[8] praising the great Florentine poet's ability to enable his readers to 'not only understand the doctrine but see the picture'.[9] But Lewis was the first

Christian writer I encountered who so clearly articulated the idea that the gospel offered a 'big picture' of reality – not so much a set of doctrines to be affirmed, but more a lens through which reality was to be seen, a picture that framed our worlds of observation and experience, a gossamer web that held together the multiple elements of our world. Other readers of Lewis had, of course, noticed this before me. The Oxford philosopher Austin Farrer observed that Lewis made his readers think they were 'listening to an argument', when in reality they were being 'presented with a vision', and it was this vision (rather than the argument) that they found compelling.[10] Where I had once regarded Christianity as primitively world-renouncing, I could now see it enabled me to appreciate the wonder and splendour of being alive, able to celebrate the fact that *I was here*, pondering these matters.

My reading of Lewis led me to experience a welcome illumination of a darkened landscape, the pulling of a lens into sharper focus, in which I began to see an essential aspect of the Christian faith clearly for the first time. I was not on my own in my journey of discovery but had found in Lewis a fellow traveller who could keep me company along what had been a somewhat lonely road up to this point. Lewis helped me to see that my own conversion to Christianity was like stepping into a grand picture, and discovering that I seemed to belong there. I was able to perceive the world in a new way, noticing interconnections that had eluded me. My earlier atheism, of course, had its own picture of reality, a somewhat bleak worldview that I believed to be true partly on account of its austerity. I had once inhabited that picture, holding it to be the only option for a thinking person; I now realised that our world could be pictured in other and better ways.

Like many students at Oxford in the 1970s, I had read Wittgenstein's *Philosophical Investigations*, and was particularly drawn to his striking statement that a 'picture held us captive'.[11] Wittgenstein noted that we too easily find ourselves enthralled by a 'picture' – a theory of the world that heightens our awareness of certain aspects of it, but nevertheless limits what we are able to see and prevents us from noticing or taking seriously evidence that might call this way of thinking into question. Worldviews have an inbuilt tendency to deceive and control, blunting our capacity to appreciate that alternative, possibly better, ways of seeing and understanding the world exist. We don't see things as *they* are; we see them as *we* are. To see reality as it is, we need to change or *be changed*, thus breaking free from the thrall of limiting and imprisoning beliefs that we were led to suppose were *facts*.

Many in the late 1960s saw Marxism as an empowering and illuminating worldview, a force for good in a dark and confused world. I initially shared this view, being drawn to Marxism's 'big picture' partly by its expansiveness. I found myself responding to this stimulus to mental and imaginative enlargement, which the Irish philosopher Edmund Burke described in terms of the 'sublime'. Yet while admiring Marxism's 'greatness of dimension', I came to realise that its overextended scope and aspirations to ultimate intellectual authority were actually telltale marks of its inadequate grounding in reality.

Where some – such as Arthur Koestler – abandoned belief in any 'big picture' as a consequence of their disillusionment with Marxism, I believed that more realistic and modest alternatives could be found and embraced. My flirtation with Marxism might have ended; it nevertheless left me with an enduring appreciation of the imaginative appeal of grand theories – whether political, scientific or theological – if we are to make any sense of our strange and complex world.

Lewis helped me to grasp the conceptual capaciousness of Christianity. Like a good scientific theory, it offered an intellectual framework that made sense of my observations and experiences of the world. It resonated with my interest in the philosophy of science, as I began to accept how the idea of 'visualisation' – being able to *see* our world – played an important role in the development of contemporary theories of scientific explanation.[12] To explain something is basically to be able to picture it. For Lewis, Christianity's special gift lies in illuminating what is observed and experienced.

I later realised that this approach was hinted at, though not fully developed, by another of Lewis' favourite poets, George Herbert, who used the analogy of a glass window to explore two different ways in which we might understand Christianity:

> A man that looks on glass,
> On it may stay his eye;
> Or if he pleaseth, through it pass,
> And then the heav'n espy.[13]

Herbert here contrasts two ways of engaging a window – a 'looking on' and a 'passing through'. I might *look at* a window, seeing it as an object of interest in itself, perhaps because of the intricacy of its glasswork; or I could *look through it*, thus using this window to see what lies beyond it. The second approach envisages Christianity serving as a *gateway to vision*, rather than being itself the *object of vision*. Herbert's point is that we can look *at* Christianity (perhaps by studying the Creeds or theological textbooks), or we can look *through* it, allowing it to act as a lens, a visualising gateway through which we see ourselves and our world more clearly. While Lewis made occasional use of the first approach, his preference was clearly for the second.

Lewis did not see this 'big picture' as offering a rigid and totalising account of reality however. It provided a *permissive* framework of understanding, which enabled me to grasp the coherence of reality without forcing the world into predetermined dogmatic categories. Lewis' approach did not assert the intellectual supremacy of Christianity; it merely affirmed the lesser, but arguably more significant, truth that Christianity was able to disclose and safeguard the coherence of our world, and locate its own distinctive position within this mental map.

Using this lens, I could see that what might otherwise be regarded as a patchwork quilt of disconnected pieces of fabric was actually a complex and interconnected whole held together by theoretical threads. Science remained science; it did not become a colony of Christian theology. Yet an imaginative framework was established that enabled me to envisage how a positive and critical dialogue between theology and the natural sciences was intellectually legitimate. Christianity created a heightened attentiveness towards the beauty and intricacy of the natural world, stimulated and engaged by the belief that appreciation of the order and beauty of the creation pointed to the wisdom and beauty of its creator. Christ's command to 'consider the lilies of the field' (Matthew 6.28–9) is an excellent example of the outcome of such attentiveness, paralleled in some ways by Henry Miller's remark that 'the moment one gives close attention to any thing, even a blade of grass, it becomes a mysterious, awesome, indescribably magnificent world in itself'.[14]

Earlier, I mentioned a sentence I encountered on my first serious reading of Lewis' essay 'Is Theology Poetry?': 'I believe in Christianity as I believe that the Sun has risen, not only because I see it but because by it I see everything else.'[15] I found this striking concluding statement to be imaginatively generative, evoking the image of standing on a hill before dawn, with the landscape below shrouded in shadow and mist. As the sun rises, the shadows are gradually dispelled and the mist slowly burns away, allowing the landscape to be seen with a depth and clarity that were impossible beforehand.

Nevertheless some shadows and patches of mist remain, partially obscuring the scene. We do not see with the total precision and clarity that the philosophers of the Enlightenment took to be desirable and achievable, but have to learn to live with an imperfect beholding of a complex reality. We see darkly, as a result of the limiting condition of being human. Not everything fits in with the logical precision some would like or expect. Our world is at points opaque and ambiguous, not least in relation to the question of suffering. Many feel not simply that pain and suffering are distressing, but that they are *wrong*. Surely our world is not meant to be like this? It seems imperfect, deficient, even unjust. Yet how can we draw such a conclusion, when we have no other world to compare it with, apart from those we invent in our dreams and imaginations?

Perhaps we have been misled here by our unrealistic expectations of how much sense we can make of our puzzling world, or an intolerance of uncertainty. After all, where does the belief that we should be able to explain *everything* come from? Why do we find it so difficult to live with unanswered questions? Surely this just leads to the destructive and groundless craving for certainty so characteristic of religious or metaphysical fundamentalisms? This quest for *philosophical* certainty is rooted in the aspirations of the Enlightenment, which unfortunately proved to rest on an inadequate account of human rational capacities. In his *Meditations on First Philosophy*, a manifesto of the 'Age of Reason', René Descartes set out his method for securing certain knowledge. But what if this is simply a rationalist fantasy? What if reality is inscrutable and resistant to this sort of reductive simplification? What if we simply have to learn to live with a degree of uncertainty and doubt?

My thoughts on these questions were clarified – though not resolved – by re-reading Plato's analogy of the cave, which I mentioned earlier. How can we live with only knowing darkly, and living in a shadowy world of incomplete and partial truths? Plato did not answer my questions, but he certainly stimulated my imagination, and opened up new ways of thinking about them.

16

Revisiting Plato's Cave:
On Darkness, Shadows and Light

Why do we find images and analogies so arresting and engaging? In part, the answer lies in the general human desire to *visualise* reality as a first step towards understanding it. Like many readers of Plato's *Republic*, I was drawn to his famous analogy of the prisoners trapped in an underground cave.[1] I was an eighteen-year-old atheist when I first encountered this, and it proved to be such a potent image that it has remained lodged in my imagination ever since. To recap, in *The Republic*, Socrates invites his disciple Glaucon to imagine a group of people who are chained facing the back wall of a great underground cave. Behind them, a fire is burning. People are moving about, talking to each other and holding up shapes of people and animals so that they cast shadows on the cave wall. The prisoners can hear echoes of the conversations of others within the cave, but cannot understand them, as the sounds are reflected and distorted by the cave's walls. They believe that these echoes and shadows constitute reality, being unaware of a world beyond the cave that would cause these to be seen in a very different way.

There is, as might be expected, a substantial scholarly literature (and no general agreement) about Plato's agenda in developing this image, and how it might feed into contemporary discussions about the human situation.[2] In my view, the image provides a framework for reflecting on two fundamental questions. Do we know only a world of darkness and flickering shadows? And if so, how might we find our way to the real world?

We need to be clear immediately that Plato's analogy proves nothing. It is an imaginative construction, which helps us to frame and explore the question of whether this world determines what is real, or whether it is an illusion or fabrication – and if so, how a real world might be discovered and entered. This remains a significant question, which features prominently in literature and films. Miguel de Unamuno's novel *Niebla* (1914) is based on the gradual realisation on the part of the main character, Augusto, that he is actually a fictional creation written into existence by Unamuno himself. *Niebla* – the Spanish term for 'fog' or 'mist' – is a narrative in which reality and fiction merge as both character and author create themselves.[3]

In the film *The Matrix* (1999), Neo (Keanu Reeves) is trapped within a false reality created by a computer program. Neo gradually realises that his senses can be systematically deceived; he lives within an illusion. A pivotal moment within the film hangs on Morpheus (Laurence Fishburne) asking Neo the question: 'What is real?' Neo comes to understand that he only sees what he is *allowed* to see, and is blinded to the existence of a greater reality – raising the question of how he might break free from this visual prison.

So let me return to my two questions. How might we find out if there is a greater world beyond the cave? And how might we enter this world? There are three lines of exploration that can be pursued here. First, there might be some markers or signs within the cave, pointing to a greater world beyond its gloomy walls. Christianity has long insisted that the created order bears witness to its creator, in effect pointing beyond itself. The natural world, on this reading, is

studded with clues and signs that suggest that some transcendent reality might lie behind or beyond the world that
we know and inhabit. Such arguments go back to the New
Testament, particularly Paul's speech at the Areopagus in
Athens (Acts 17.16–34), and were developed more fully by
writers such as Thomas Aquinas and C.S. Lewis. These lines
of reflection are not, and never were regarded as, 'proofs' of
God's existence, but as demonstrations of the intrinsic rationality (or at least the intellectual consistency) of the Christian
faith. Such clues include the mysterious rational transparency
and unnecessary beauty of the universe, and the capacity of
mathematics to mirror the structures of our world.

In the second place, the prisoners within the cave might
have some deep intuition that this was not their true home,
and come to believe that they belonged somewhere else. They
might experience a sense of longing for something that nothing within the cave is able to satisfy, or sense that there has to
be more than this limited world. (I remember well some
words a colleague once used in describing his religious awak-
ening: 'I felt that I was made for somewhere else'.) Our quest
for fulfilment often leads us to attach ourselves to objects or
persons in this world, as C.S. Lewis noted, only to discover
that these were actually signposts to something that lay
beyond them, rather than being the source of joy and meaning in themselves: 'It was not *in* them, it only came *through*
them, and what came through them was longing'.[4] For Lewis,
the Christian understanding of the meaning of life makes
sense of human experiences of moral obligation and beauty,
in that both have their origin and goal in God.

Now these are *clues*, not *proofs*; they gain their force
through a cumulative resonance with the intellectual frameworks within which they are located. On their own, they

prove nothing; they are a set of observations that we have to try and fit within various possible intellectual frameworks, including the Christian 'big picture'. What 'big picture', then, makes the most sense of these clues? What metanarrative offers the best map of reality, positioning observations in the most comprehensive and plausible manner? How well does the theory fit these accumulated observations? Would these observations be *expected* if this picture is reliable? Some of the forms of Platonism and Gnosticism that were prevalent in late classical antiquity could certainly cope with a number of these clues, particularly the sense that this world is not where we ultimately belong. But not all of them.

Moreover, there is a third intriguing possibility: someone from the outside world enters the shadowy confines of the cave, speaking of what lies beyond, and offering to lead those trapped in the cavernous gloom into this as yet unknown bright sunlit realm. This is about more than informing or persuading people that there is a world beyond the cave; it is about removing obstacles and barriers to *discerning* and *entering* that world. To use the language of Christian theology, to discover and inhabit the reality beyond the cave requires both *revelation* and *redemption*.

Plato asks us to imagine someone who escapes from that cave and enters the sunlit world that lies beyond. Even though she is initially overwhelmed by the radiance of the sun, she is able to appreciate the beauty and wonder of this strange new realm, and contrast it with the lesser existence she knew from the cave. For Plato, a philosopher is someone who has seen this greater vision of reality and returns to the cave to tell others of what she has seen and how it enables a proper understanding of reality. Yet because the philosopher now has a greater clarity of vision through her encounter with the external world, her audience within the cave finds her vision difficult to grasp and accept; they cannot see what she has seen. Their imaginative representations of the world need to be expanded and enlarged if they are to accommodate the greater reality, for which their experience of the cave has failed to prepare them.

Early Christian writers found Plato a congenial dialogue partner, noting that he shared their belief in a transcendent realm that illuminated and informed our life in this world. Christian theology uses the category of revelation to denote an expanded vision of what constitutes 'the real'. We are offered a clarity of vision that arises from beyond the limits of our human situation, enabling us to see our situation and our possibilities as they really are, and thus challenging our presuppositions about ourselves and our world.

The Christian 'big picture' – as set out, for example, by Augustine of Hippo – includes a somewhat sober assessment of the limits of human vision and action. We do not see clearly; nor do we possess the capacity to break free from self-absorption and self-delusion. We may know what we ought to be doing; that in itself does not mean that we *wish* to do it, or that we *can* do it. Christianity depicts human nature as wounded, damaged, broken and frail, prone to error and delusion. Education is not enough; something more than mere information is needed in order to heal our wounds and restore us to wholeness. What we see and do is determined by what we are; to see and act properly, we must be changed.

Theologically, the transformative impact of the Christian gospel upon individuals is often articulated using medical models. Augustine made extensive use of medical images in exploring the many aspects of the Christian gospel. God's grace restored people to wholeness, offering a salve for their wounds. Augustine thus argued that the Christian Church could be conceived as a hospital – a place in which wounded and broken people might receive care and healing.

Augustine's analysis is an important corrective to anyone who might think of Christianity offering *only* a 'big picture' of human beings and the world. While this grand vision identifies the problem, it then moves on to articulate how our situation might be changed and transformed. For Christians, Christ is the 'light of the world' who illuminates both our situation and the path we should take, and the 'good shepherd' who accompanies us as we travel through this dark and puzzling world. He is the trailblazer, the 'pioneer and perfecter of our faith' (Hebrews 12.2) who has gone ahead of us, to show us what lies beyond the cave, and allow us to follow along the path he has created. Christ is the 'Word made flesh' (John 1.14), God incarnate who has entered into a fallen and created world to illuminate and transform our situation.

Plato's analogy of the cave naturally focuses our attention on how we might live in such a shadowy world, in which we see darkly and imperfectly. But how can we cope with such ambiguity, when we long for total clarity? This seems to me to be the epistemic tragedy of humanity – longing to know what cannot be known with certainty, and thus having to do the best we can to make sense of this world, and our place within it.

I have come to admire the Irish writer John Banville, who captures something of this precariousness and fragility of our knowledge of what really matters. 'What a little vessel of strangeness we are, sailing through this muffled silence through the autumn dark.'[5] Some make uncertainty into a fetish – 'we can know nothing'. Yet this extreme scepticism ultimately rests on a certainty – that nothing can be known. I simply draw the more realistic conclusion that we are *entitled* to believe, yet are often unable to provide totally compelling and conclusive reasons for what we believe. As I have become older, I have accepted that I must not merely *live* with this difficult truth, but *work* with it, realising that this leaves many unanswered questions and unresolved issues. That is perhaps the most difficult lesson I have had to learn.

17

Longing for Certainty:
Proof, Faith and Doubt

I was drawn to the natural sciences in the slipstream of my early love of nature. Anyone who knows the exquisite sense of wonder evoked by the vastness and beauty of the natural world will understand how that sense of rapturous delight transposes organically into a yearning to understand and appreciate the mysteries of nature. Yet looking back on my teenage love of science, I now see there was another influence at work – my inability to cope with uncertainty. I believed that science was about *facts* – objective truths that could be proved to be right, resting on unshakeable experimental evidence. I would simply have been baffled by the philosopher Alasdair MacIntyre's famous quip that 'facts, like telescopes and wigs for gentlemen, were a seventeenth-century invention'.[1]

As a teenager, I surrounded myself with a protective steel cage of certainties, perhaps as a way of coping with the disquietingly uncertain implications of a dramatically changing social and political situation in Belfast in the late 1960s. Heraclitus had argued that everything changes and nothing lasts for ever. But recognising the inevitability of change did not help me cope with uncertainty about the specific form this might take. What would remain of the past? What would the future look life?

Like the Stoics, I sought refuge from a transient and unpredictable social world by constructing a secure and stable realm within my mind, grounded in the certainties of reason and science, into which I could retreat for security and comfort. I was morbidly averse to uncertainty, and craved certainty and the elimination of doubt in my convictions.[2] The Greek philosopher Xenophanes argued that philosophy was a 'woven web of guesses'. Happily, I told myself, science allowed us to move on from this pessimism, which had been corrected by scientific progress and the 'Age of Reason'. In my view, doubt was an existentially distressing epistemic vice, which was fortunately rendered unnecessary by a rational and scientific view of the world. Doubt was only a problem for those with a religious disposition; science stood above this, being able to establish its convictions with certainty.

While I was studying for A Level physics and chemistry at Methody, I took the view (which I later discovered to be characteristic of the writings of Richard Dawkins) that science *proved* its ideas, so that faith was both unnecessary and inappropriate for a natural scientist. Since science is based on evidence, faith is superfluous and doubt is eliminated, in that evidence convinces us of the truth with compelling clarity.[3] There was no need to engage primitive pre-scientific philosophies, which were painfully ignorant of this evidence-based approach to reasoning.

Methody's library became my place of security, a book-lined fortress of eternal evidence-based certainties that shielded me from the ephemeral and unpredictable world of a socially fragmenting Belfast beyond the library's walls. Perhaps that was why my close reading of works dealing with the history and philosophy of science in early 1971 was so traumatic. My secure intellectual world was corroded from within – by the very books that were meant to protect me. There was a traitor within the citadel of reason, whispering words of doubt.

When I was ten, I loved science because it engaged my sense of wonder at nature; when I was sixteen, I loved science for its deliverance of certainties in the midst of cultural anxiety and insecurity. Like most teenagers in British schools, I had been taught to think of science as 'dogma – a set of unequivocal, uncontested and unquestioned facts'.[4] Yet this set of certainties was crumbling away, as my knowledge base increased. Why did science change its mind on so many things? Why did science once tell people that the universe was eternal, only to backtrack and tell them it actually had a beginning? Science is characterised by a long succession of falsified theories in the past – think of phlogiston and caloric, well-regarded in their day yet now discarded. It became impossible for me to avoid being sceptical about what science *presently* believed to be right. Which of its current theories would be discarded or superseded in the future? Science was, I reasoned, a set of provisional conclusions, only some of which would stand the test of time.

This was an unsettling thought, but I grudgingly conceded that it made a lot more sense of the history of science than the triumphant linear narrative of progress that characterised my scientific positivism at the time. I later read Michael Polanyi's *Personal Knowledge* (1958), which explored the somewhat disquieting implications of the scientific necessity of a personal commitment to something which might well turn out to be false, yet had to be embraced in trust. This line of thought did not make me a sceptic or a relativist; it did, however, subvert the naivety of a young scientist who knew nothing about the history or philosophy of the scientific enterprise, sowing the seeds of doubt about alleged scientific 'certainties'. As a result, I began to think of science as a process that delivered provisional conclusions on the basis of robust evidential criteria, but whose future beliefs could not be predicted. What was believed in the present might be radically modified or abandoned in the future.

Yet the seeds of doubt that were sown in the spring of 1971 related to more than the nature and scope of science. I was beginning to have doubts about the reliability of human reason. Even though I suppressed these as best I could, they kept resurfacing and multiplying, like the heads of the Hydra in Euripides' account of the labours of Hercules. The persistent thought that I failed to suppress or extinguish was that the world of logical and philosophical certainties was a closed and isolated mental compartment, a tidy, watertight construction of the human mind that failed to connect up with the perplexing and messy real world which lay beyond my head, and within which I had to live. It was easy for me to assemble a list of indubitable certainties from the disciplines of logic and mathematics, such as $2 + 2 = 4$, or 'the whole is greater than the part'. But these somehow seemed trivial and insignificant, prompting the destructively dismissive retort, 'So what?'

I still believed that religion was uniquely irrational in that it depended on an unevidenced 'leap of faith'. Yet I was becoming uneasy about this judgement. Was religion really on its own in wanting to go beyond what reason could prove? Like David Hume before me, I simply could not see how *any* ethical or political beliefs were compatible with the scientific method. Surely scientists ought to be ethical people though? In order to be consistent, was I duty-bound to abandon ethics and politics as areas of human thought that were incompatible with scientific reasoning?

I used to think that atheism was factually correct, so that anyone who believed in God had to make a case for clinging on to what was clearly an irrational belief. Belief in God, however, is only irrational from a particular point of view – that of atheism. This judgement represents one viewpoint assessing another, each dependent on certain fundamental assumptions that cannot be proved right. I now see both atheism and religious faith as personal judgements which go beyond the available evidence. This does not mean that either of them is wrong; it simply means that they both represent *beliefs* – and hence that, since they cannot be proved, they are uncertain.

It became disturbingly clear to me that the pathway from evidence to truth was rather more complex than I had imagined, involving a leap of faith in arriving at *any* belief, rather than a rationally continuous and logically seamless progression from *observation of the world* to the *construction of a worldview*. My atheism seemed increasingly to be an under-evidenced and over-confident hypothesis, an invitation to live as if there was no God, while being unable to prove this premise was right. An inconvenient (if courageous) leap of faith was required on my part from the ambiguity of the world to the nothingness of the beyond, which I disguised by pretending that atheism was exempt from the critical reasoning it used against its opponents.

Such deliberations were propelling me towards the erosion of rational and scientific certainty. Fortunately, I began to realise that what I initially feared as a catastrophe might well turn out to be the beginning of a new and more reliable way of thinking in which I would no longer need to suppress the doubts of 1971. And with that thought in mind, I went to Oxford, believing that its rich intellectual environment would help me sort myself out.

At Oxford, I was able to follow through on the suspicions of my late teenage years, and discovered them to be subversive – not of *truth*, but rather of a deficient and indefensible *understanding of truth*, which was inattentive to both the complexity of the world and the limits of human reasoning. I was able to read works dealing with the philosophy of science more thoroughly, and find a navigable path through this conceptual maze to a way of thinking that I could take seriously. This involved temporary attachments to philosophers whom I found helpful in some respects (such as John Locke, David Hume and José Ortega y Gasset) and more enduring engagements with others (such as Ludwig Wittgenstein, C.S. Peirce, Iris Murdoch and Mary Midgley). I remain convinced that, providing that their limits are recognised and respected, the natural sciences remain the most reliable source of human knowledge of our world. Yet even in the natural sciences, theories are frequently underdetermined by evidence,[5] in that a body of observations is often open to multiple interpretations, generating debate about which criteria should be used to evaluate which is to be seen as the 'best' such interpretation, and whether the *best* explanation is necessarily the *right* explanation. 'Proof', in the proper sense of the term, is limited to the closed worlds of logic and mathematics, and that in every other area of life human beings have to come to terms with accepting ideas that cannot be proven, but may nonetheless be considered to be trustworthy or reliable.

The American philosopher C.S. Peirce made an interesting comparison on this point between the natural sciences and criminal trials. In both cases, an array of observational evidence is presented, with a view to finding what seems to be the best explanation of this evidence. In neither case, however, can this be proved to be right with *logical* precision. Peirce's point is given added force by David Hume's critique of induction – the approach to reasoning that lies behind most natural sciences.[6] Some philosophers consider Hume's argument to be unassailable, entailing an 'inductive scepticism' that holds that inductive inferences cannot be justified.

While Hume's concerns have never been convincingly refuted, however, most natural scientists seem quite happy to live and work with these unresolved issues. Charles Darwin, while noting Hume's concerns, makes the pragmatic point that science still works perfectly well despite this Humean uncertainty.[7] Darwin's point has helped inform my own reflections: theoretical uncertainty does not prevent us from making pragmatic decisions about our lives and beliefs.

This point is reinforced by the case of Bertrand Russell, who spoke of philosophy helping us to live with uncertainty. While he is sometimes spoken of as an 'atheist' philosopher, Russell explicitly identifies himself as an *agnostic*, in that he regarded the question of God as lying beyond proof.[8] His epistemological agnosticism is often overlooked by those who simplistically classify him as an atheist, thus aligning him with the glib certainties asserted by Richard Dawkins.[9] Russell took the view that he could live *as if* there were no God, despite being unable to show that this was the case. Russell was thus prepared to allow that he was an atheist in the *popular* sense of that term, thus distinguishing his epistemological agnosticism from his pragmatic atheism.

Russell helped me to see something that I now regard as obvious: that human beings can, and do, live on the basis of certain convictions – including both Christianity and atheism – that they hold to be meaningful and trustworthy, despite not being able to demonstrate that they are true. Karl Popper introduced the phrase 'ultimate questions' to designate the big questions about the meaning of life and the nature of the good that really matter to people, yet which cannot be proved to be true by any known scientific means. Any answer to such 'ultimate questions' in the end amounts to a matter of *what is believed* rather than *what can be proved*.

One such 'ultimate question' concerns the meaning of life. In her autobiographical memoir, Jeanette Winterson points out how a quest for a deeper meaning and higher purpose seems to be hard-wired within us, making us dissatisfied with purely functional accounts of ourselves and our world.

> We cannot simply eat, sleep, hunt and reproduce – we are meaning seeking creatures. The Western world has done away with religion but not with our religious impulses; we seem to need some higher purpose, some point to our lives – money and leisure, social progress, are just not enough.[10]

To be human is to ask recognisably *religious* questions. Yet the answers that are given to these questions cannot be proved to be true or false. They take the form of a working hypothesis, a belief that Polanyi described as 'personal judgment', and the philosopher of science Bas van Fraassen as a 'stance'.[11]

I have always been puzzled that leading writers of the New Atheism that briefly and noisily made its appearance in 2006–7 – such as Christopher Hitchens and Richard Dawkins – insisted that they have no 'beliefs' and only accepted what can be proved to be true. Hitchens' scatter-shot verbal brilliance in his *God is not Great* (2007) obscures the fact that his outlook on life is that of the eighteenth century, serenely undisturbed by recent seismic shifts in the philosophy of science that have forced the rest of us to move away from the naive rationalism of this bygone 'Age of Reason' *on rational grounds*.

A critical reading of Hitchens' and Dawkins' works shows their arguments rely at crucial points on cultural and philosophical assumptions that clearly lie beyond proof. Hitchens and Dawkins seem to assume that their readers will share those assumptions, thus exempting them from the process of critical interrogation that these authors direct against theists, yet unfortunately fail to apply to their own beliefs. While these hopeless overstatements initially received a remarkably uncritical reception by sympathetic secular cultural commentators, their vulnerability is now widely conceded.

Dawkins seems to think that evidence leads unproblematically to the deduction of scientific theories, which can be treated as factual statements. 'Good supporting evidence' renders faith 'superfluous', in that 'the evidence would compel us to believe it anyway'.[12] This is the commonsense view of someone who has yet to encounter and assimilate the history and philosophy of science, above all, the critical distinction between a 'logic of discovery' and a 'logic of justification'. Even the best 'supporting evidence' is open to several interpretations, so that establishing criteria for theory choice is of critical importance. Yet there is still no fundamental agreement on what those criteria might be, which are to be given precedence, and the theoretical basis determining why (or whether) these criteria are to be adopted in the first place.

As Karl Popper points out, scientific knowledge is best seen as provisional, conjectural and hypothetical. It could be said that we are all agnostics, in some sense and to some degree – a point that Richard Dawkins belatedly appears to have conceded in his 2012 Oxford debate with Rowan Williams. It is one thing to prove shallow truths; yet, as Popper pointed out, the beliefs in life that really matter lie beyond logical or scientific proof. Doubt and uncertainty are hard-wired into all but our most superficial engagements with the universe.

This tolerance of uncertainty as a hallmark of the human situation is perhaps one of the most distinct divergences between my older and younger self. Some might despair at this situation, grumbling about the cruel disjunction between what we *can* know and what we *want* to know. Yet, as Milan Kundera observed, we need to appreciate the importance of asking and exploring 'questions with no answers', which help us probe our limits as human beings,[13] challenging us to take intellectual risks in transgressing the boundaries of a cold and sterile rationalism.

Theoretically, we ought not to be able to arrive at settled beliefs; *pragmatically*, we do this all the time. I have learned to live with this tension – namely, believing that I have good reasons for holding a belief that I consider to be important and meaningful, yet knowing it cannot be proved. Perhaps this is a truth we need to embrace gladly. It is, after all, *liberating*, in that it sets us free from the demand to prove the unprovable, and allows us to get on with the serious business of living as best we can in the light of what we believe we are justified in valuing and trusting.

18

Delusion: Faith as Wish-Fulfilment?

One of my most strident imagined certainties as a teenager studying science at Methody in the late 1960s was that belief in God was a psychological crutch, a consoling belief for sad human beings who were incapable of coping with the brutal reality of a godless, meaningless universe. God was a reassuring fabrication, a delusion spun out of irrational hopes and pitiable aspirations. Religious belief was infantile and would inevitably give way to the maturity of atheism.

Although I had not read anything by Sigmund Freud at this stage, my progressive atheist student friends at Queen's University Belfast talked a lot about his idea of 'wish-fulfilment', which they regarded as a knock-down argument against religion. The desire for the kind of consolation that God might provide created the false (though understandable) belief that there was a God. I liked this argument, and perhaps for that reason failed to follow it through with the analytical precision that its boldness and scope demanded.

I was intellectually arrogant and personally insecure at this time, and dealt with both of these problems by aligning myself with the intellectually progressive movements of the age. I persuaded myself that this was 'freethinking', when it was little more than a passive acceptance of the beliefs of cultural in-groups. This strategy satisfied my need to be socially accepted, to be seen as part of an intelligent cultural elite and bask in its reflected glory. Hanging out with students at Queen's University while I was still in the sixth form at Methody was really a quest for validation or accept-ance within an older peer group.

Embracing Christianity put an end to my narcissistic longing for validation and acceptance, which could easily have become a destructive introversion. The Christian doctrine of justification by faith, of which I knew nothing at that stage, spoke of being accepted by God as the ground of true self-esteem. I did not need to achieve to be loved; rather, I needed to accept that I was valued by God, and so could get on with life without the need for constant reassurance. Having resolved this matter, I went on to research and write an exhaustive history of this Christian doctrine, and its impact on Christian life and thought.[1]

Freud was still regarded as an unassailable cultural authority in Belfast in the late 1960s, long before it became clear just how many of his core 'scientific' ideas were founded on limited and disputed evidence, leading to unfal-sifiable conclusions. At this time, Freud was widely regarded as the 'Darwin of the Mind', a progressive scientist who outraged the religious establishment by exposing the disturb-ing ease with which human beings invent God to meet their subconscious existential and psychological needs. Snappy slogans – such as 'science proves that belief in God is an illu-sion' – trumped serious argument in the student circles I knew. It was taken as a self-evident truth that atheism was the only option for a freethinking and scientifically informed person like myself.

I considered atheism to be an act of intellectual boldness, in that this belief offered no 'metaphysical comfort' (Nietzsche), but only a bleak and harsh interpretation of a meaningless world. I came to the view that the aesthetic deficit and existential drabness of atheism were reliable indications of its truth: who would *want* to believe something so unattractive and dull? There was no danger of atheism arising from wish-fulfilment!

Looking back on those days from where I now stand, I can see that while I was *rightly* suspicious of any arguments about God based on human desire, I was *selectively* suspicious. I was justified in having concerns that I might create a worldview that simply mirrored my own desires of what the world ought to be like. But I selectively applied this only to belief in God, failing to recognise that it also applied to my emerging atheism. In hindsight, I can now see something that I conspicuously failed to appreciate in those bygone days. *I didn't want there to be a God*. I wanted to be in control of my life, and saw any transcendent authority as a threat to my self-preoccupied and self-regulated world. Was this why I criticised risible caricatures of Christianity, yet failed to talk to Christians to discover what they really believed? Might I have embraced atheism in order to neutralise a potential challenge to my self-centred and self-referential world?

I would not be the first to have done so. The philosopher Thomas Nagel, whose thinking I engage appreciatively in my recent writings, was quite explicit about the fundamental motivation for his atheism. 'It isn't just that I don't believe in God, and, naturally, hope that I'm right in my belief. It's that I hope there is no God! I don't want there to be a God; I don't want the universe to be like that.'[2] The wish here gives rise to the belief; Nagel's atheism seems to be a *post hoc* rationalisation of his more fundamental desire for a godless universe.

Similarly, the biologist Aldous Huxley made it clear that he rejected belief in God for motives that had little to do with science or reason, inventing arguments to justify his atheism after he had adopted it. 'I had motives for not wanting the world to have a meaning; consequently assumed that it had none, and was able without any difficulty to find satisfying reasons for this assumption.'[3] Other examples of this process could easily be given, such as those who reject belief in God for reasons of personal taste ('I find religion offensive') or social prejudice ('religious people are so *vulgar*') or cultural status ('no intelligent person could believe in God'). Covert social and emotional factors drive our decision-making more than we care to admit.

Happily, discussion of these issues has moved on since the austerely rationalist frameworks of the 1960s. We are now much more alert to the way in which emotional and volitional issues cloud and shape what many had assumed to be the objective and detached worlds of philosophy and the natural sciences. Nagel's atheism amounts to a retrospective intellectual validation of a belief that had actually been determined on emotional grounds – a good example of what the psychologist Jonathan Haidt more recently described as the 'emotional tail' wagging the 'rationalist dog'.[4] People reach conclusions on intuitive or emotional grounds, and later figure out justifications for those beliefs. This uncomfortable insight needs to be woven into any account of moral, political, religious and anti-religious ideas. Our thinking about science, politics and religion all too often reflects what we *want* to be the case, so that we determine (and perhaps even *invent*) highly selective rational justifications later.[5] Too easily, we reject an option because we don't like it, not because it is intellectually flawed.

While the danger of inventing worlds and worldviews to suit our tastes, agendas and desires must be recognised, this does not in itself invalidate such beliefs. Desires often emerge in response to something we require for our survival or well-being. I do not know anyone who holds that, because hunger reflects a human need, it is to be regarded as an illusion. Our longing for significance might well be a clue to human identity, corresponding to some deep, existential need which helps us appreciate who we really are. What we *desire* may well disclose who we *are*.

Whether a belief is 'rational' or not depends on the assumed informing context, in that such feelings or desires are *interpreted* within a preconceived intellectual framework. An atheist ideology – such as that presupposed (yet certainly not proved) by Freud or Marx – can only interpret a 'longing for God' on the basis of the controlling assumption that there is no God. This longing must therefore be seen as a delusion, in that it can have no objective basis. This *interpretation* is thus in turn dependent upon a *belief*, which is itself incapable of verification or falsification.

A Christian way of thinking, however, holds that human beings bear the 'image of God', and for that reason, long for God. The famous prayer of Augustine of Hippo makes this point well: 'You have made us for yourself, and our heart is restless until it finds its rest in you'. With this view, we have an inbuilt longing for God, which may temporarily attach itself to lesser goods in the course of its quests, but in the end finds these inadequate and continues to search for its true source and goal. For Augustine, this sense of longing is thus not a delusion, but a clue to our true identity and a pointer to how we might ultimately satisfy our heart's desire. Once more, this interpretation is dependent upon a belief, which is incapable of verification or falsification. We are not being asked to choose between a Christian 'faith' and an atheist 'fact', but between two divergent and equally unverified interpretive frameworks.

The epistemic dilemma we face as informed human beings is that we feel the need to commit ourselves to beliefs that we consider to be important, even life-changing, but are unable to prove are true. We might indeed wish that we could inhabit a world of certainties; sadly, that is increasingly being seen as a delusion, which, if taken seriously, leads us to commit intellectual violence in order to shore up these discredited beliefs in the face of disconfirming evidence.

So how do we deal with this dilemma? I have learned much on this from the writings of the Oxford intellectual historian and philosopher Sir Isaiah Berlin. In his famous lecture of 1988 'The Pursuit of the Ideal', Berlin offered a philosophical demolition of those who 'have, by their own methods, arrived at clear and unshakeable convictions about what to do and what to be that brook no possible doubt'.[6] Berlin was scathing about the foundations and implications of such epistemic arrogance, which amounted to little more than wish-fulfilment: 'I can only say that those who rest on such comfortable beds of dogma are victims of forms of self-induced myopia, blinkers that make for contentment, but not for understanding of what it is to be human'.

Berlin believed that the Western philosophical tradition, particularly during the 'Age of Reason', had been seduced by the possibility of discovering a single, rational hierarchy of human values. This, Berlin declared, was demonstrably wrong; we need to recognise a plurality of rationally defensible understandings of values, which were often inconsistent with each other, raising the question of how we can live alongside those who come to very different conclusions through reasoned reflection.[7] Berlin's experience of Logical

Positivism in Oxford during the 1930s led him to conclude that, while the scientific method is essential to our understanding of the natural world, it was incorrect to apply this to fundamental questions of value and meaning. Although these cannot be verified scientifically or logically, they are essential to human life and culture.

If Berlin is right, we must learn to be respectful of those who take divergent positions on these matters, precisely because these reasoned judgements, though capable of rational justification, lie beyond final proof. Our world is so complex, and is interpreted within the parameters of so many competing visions of rationality, that disagreement between intelligent and informed people is *inevitable*, even if we might hope it might also be *respectful*. So how do we try and engage such a complex reality? One answer is to try to map our world of ideas.

19

Maps of Reality: Coping with the Complexity of Our World

In 2006, I received an invitation to give the 2008 Riddell Memorial Lectures at the University of Newcastle in the north-east of England. I was delighted by this invitation, not least because C.S. Lewis had delivered those same lectures in 1942.[1] I was due to explore some aspects of natural theology. The title I chose for these lectures was based on a phrase from Isaac Newton: 'Standing on the Shore of the Ocean of Truth'.[2] A few weeks before I was due to give my lectures in February 2008, I received an invitation to have tea with the philosopher Mary Midgley, who had been a lecturer at Newcastle until her retirement in 1980. Since then, she had remained in Newcastle, and authored a number of well-received books, many of which were critical of reductionist accounts of human nature. I naturally accepted her invitation, and looked forward to our conversation.

We met after I had given an additional lecture on the topic of Richard Dawkins' interesting opinions on the rationality of religion, which the lecture committee had invited me to give in view of strong local interest in the topic. Midgley and I were allowed to use a common room in the Law Building, where I had given the lecture, and were provided with some tea and rather splendid biscuits by university staff, who clearly regarded Midgley as a local heroine.

I cannot really describe what followed as a conversation; it was more akin to a forensic interrogation, in which Midgley

dissected my views on the use of analogies in scientific thinking, a cup of tea perched precariously on her knee, wobbling
alarmingly as she gesticulated to make her points. Her main
target was Dawkins' notion of the 'selfish gene'. How, she
asked, could genes be 'selfish'? It made as much sense as
suggesting that atoms were jealous. Despite my differences
with him, I defended Dawkins here, pointing out that he
made it clear he was using the word 'selfish' as a kind of
shorthand, a way of expressing his observation that genes
behave *as if* they were selfish. Midgley was not impressed: her
response included the word 'fiddlesticks!' and a noise which I
am told should be written down as 'harrumphing'.

We soon got on to more constructive themes, including
the question of how we could represent reality without
reductive distortion. On this point, we reached agreement: it
was important to find a way of identifying and safeguarding
the multiple aspects of complex realities. Midgley used the
language of multiple 'conceptual toolboxes' to make the
point that we need to use different methods of research,
each adapted to a specific task, in order to investigate the
world. While I myself preferred the simpler term 'research
methods', I was impressed by the richness and accessibility
of Midgley's image of the 'toolbox' or 'toolkit', and decided
to start using it myself (while naturally acknowledging its
venerable source).

I explained how I found the language of 'multiple perspectives' helpful, and confessed that I had borrowed this idea
from Charles Coulson; Midgley countered with her own preference for 'multiple maps', and gave some examples of how
she used this analogy.[3] The point she wanted me to appreciate
was that different maps provide different information about
the same reality. Once more, I realised that Midgley's image

was imaginatively productive, and asked her if she would mind if I started using it myself once I had figured out some ways of applying it to theological contexts. Midgley thought this was an obvious and entirely appropriate thing to do. While she did not share my Christian faith, she kindly described it as 'perfectly sensible'. We parted as friends.

Midgley needs to be heard, in the face of those who aggressively and dismissively insist that there is only one valid way of exploring and representing our complex world. This reductive simplification is the inevitable outcome of a theory-driven reading of the world that is more concerned to validate itself than to understand our strange universe. I had taken this view myself back in the 1960s, believing that reality was limited to what the natural sciences could reveal and confirm, yet failing to grasp that I had actually limited reality to what this single research method could disclose.

My liberation from this self-imposed deception came mainly through my studies of quantum mechanics and the philosophy of science at Oxford. Werner Heisenberg insisted that 'what we observe is not nature itself, but nature as it is disclosed by our methods of investigation'.[4] The more research methods we employ, the better our rendering of the natural world. Science is not a monolithic practice, defined by a single method; rather, it consists of a constellation of individual sciences with specific research methods that have been developed and adapted over time with their specific research goals in mind. We need to respect the integrities of these different disciplines, as opposed to trying to force them into the same mould for ideological reasons.

John Habgood, a Cambridge research scientist who eventually became Archbishop of York, appreciated the importance of this point. He remarked that the use of 'science' in the singular, or a persistent reference to '*the* scientific method', failed to do justice to the methodological diversity that is so clearly observed and practised within and across the natural sciences. This habit of speaking, Habgood suggests, may be traced back to the establishment of the British Association for the Advancement of Science in 1831.[5] In its understandable desire to avoid the fragmentation of individual natural sciences, the founders of the British Association chose to speak simply of 'science' – and in doing so, created the expectation that there was a singular method and outlook that was distinctive of all such natural sciences, namely, 'the scientific method'.

Habgood thus argued for the retrieval of the older idea of a 'spectrum of sciences', developing 'disciplines of study appropriate to their subject matter' (what Midgley called 'toolboxes'), and then finding a way of weaving these multiple threads of insight into a patterned tapestry. Within a Christian perspective, Habgood insisted, the fundamental interconnectedness and coherence of reality can be affirmed and held together within a web of meaning.

An undivided mind looks in the end for an undivided truth, a oneness at the heart of things. And this isn't just fantasy. The whole intellectual quest, despite its fragmentation, despite its limitations and uncertainties, seems to presuppose that in the end we are all encountering a single reality, and a single truth.[6]

Midgley made a similar point, championing philosophical resistance to the narrowing of our hearts and constriction of our minds, stressing that the quality of our thinking ought to be as deep and complex as the world that we hope to understand. Midgley's idea of requiring and developing 'multiple maps' of nature seemed to have potential value in exploring how the many aspects of a 'single reality' can be distinguished, while continuing to see them as inseparable from the greater whole. It seemed to me to be like passing a beam of white light through a prism, and observing how it was separated out into the colours of the rainbow: red, orange, yellow, green, blue, indigo and violet. All those colours were present in the original beam of white light; the prism merely allowed them to be seen and appreciated individually.

Mapping a complex terrain is about presenting a range of information about the same reality. A physical map of Europe shows us the features of the landscape. A political map, however, shows the borders of its nation states. Each map is designed to answer a specific set of questions; the physical map supplements, without displacing, the political map. Each map makes sense of the whole landscape by presenting certain specific information about it – and not others. To get an overall view of this complex terrain, we need to find some way of superimposing these multiple maps, so that all this information may be displayed and integrated.

This is an especially important point in considering the relation of science and faith, to which I shall return in the following chapter. Science maps how our world works; faith maps what it means. These two maps thus complement each other, allowing a richer understanding of the world they represent. One map helps us to understand our world, and how it works; the other helps us to understand our true nature and destiny, and why we are here. We need both maps to inhabit this world meaningfully.

We need scientific, ethical, political, social and religious maps to help us navigate our way through the landscape of our world. No one map is able to answer all our questions. We are right to resist those who demand we acknowledge the sole legitimacy of their map of reality, which discloses only what they wish us to know. As history makes clear, the construction of a map often represents the assertion of power, involving claims to total authority over a geographical region – or an intellectual field.

Yet mapping also serves another purpose. Many regard science and religion as being in conflict on the basis of a flawed conceptual map of their possible relationships. The Australian intellectual historian Peter Harrison has exposed the critical role played by such maps, which determine whether the disciplines of science and religion are to be seen as conflicting or enriching.[7] For Harrison, the boundaries on this particular map are to be seen as social constructions, not empirical observations. The map we use determines what we see – for example, whether science and religion compete for the same territory, or occupy adjacent yet disconnected territories. Too often, we fail to realise that some maps are drawn up for political and polemical purposes.

In my 2008 conversation with Mary Midgley, I remarked that her notion of 'multiple maps' might be useful theologically, and went on to explore its potential – for example, in trying to grasp and express the significance of Jesus Christ. Midgley's way of thinking not only helped me to make sense of my own faith; it allowed me to explain it to those who found the traditional metaphysical understandings of the 'Two Natures' of Christ somewhat baffling.

I do not myself find the metaphysical statements in the Nicene Creed (such as Christ 'being of one substance' with

God) particularly problematic. As I see the development of early Christian theology, they were translations or transpositions of the language of the New Testament into the culturally dominant conceptual framework of Hellenistic philosophy. That transposition worked well in Late Classical Antiquity, and served as a defining landmark in the crystallisation of the Christian understanding of the identity and significance of Christ, and an informing resource for subsequent theological reflection. It now needed to be interpreted to a new generation, by being restated or repositioned within frameworks that resonated with the cultural mood of our present day. Midgley's idea of 'mapping' gave me a tool that helped me to do this.

The Creeds do not present Jesus Christ as an abstract theological principle but as a real historical figure who transcends the limits of any and all historical contexts – a person, not an abstraction or a disembodied idea. To appreciate his importance, we need to use several maps of meaning. No single map is adequate to the task of disclosing what the New Testament calls the 'boundless riches of Christ' (Ephesians 3.8).

The idea of 'multiple maps' is useful historically. Think of Julius Caesar leading an army across the River Rubicon in 49 BC. A physical map shows us where this river was located; yet a *political* map tells us that it marked a frontier. By crossing this river, Caesar was declaring war against the Roman republic. We need both those maps to understand the significance of that event. Or think of the death of Christ. We can use historical and geographical maps to make sense of some of its aspects. But to understand its decisive impact on the Christian faith, we also need to use a *theological* map. Christ did not simply die; he died *for our sins* (1 Corinthians 15.3).

Midgley's approach can, of course, be extended further, not least in relation to understanding the rich Christian interpretations of salvation. What difference does Christ make to us? We can map out a complex yet reliable response, framing the New Testament's images of salvation (often known as 'soteriological metaphors') in terms of relational fulfilment and restoration, forgiveness of sin, the healing of wounded and broken people, the giving of a new identity, or the creation of hope – to mention only a few themes, to which more can easily be added.

Even though I have only offered a very brief sketch of how Midgley's approach can be used theologically, I think enough has been said to enable further exploration. To go back to an image that I have always found helpful, we need maps of the landscape of faith to enable us to find our way around, and to know what to look for. Complexity is to be welcomed, being seen as a sign of richness, rather than as something that must be reduced to some simplistic slogan or abstract principle. Midgley's approach helps me to affirm the basic unity and coherence of our world and the Christian faith, while at the same time mapping its rich individual themes, and highlighting specific threads of thought.

Moreover, Midgley's approach also helped me consolidate my understanding of the relation of science and faith – perhaps one of the most important questions I was forced to confront in both my personal journey of faith, and my professional career.

20

Science and Faith: Conflicting or Enriching?

In September 2008, I took up the Professorship of Theology, Ministry and Education at King's College London. My office overlooked the south bank of the Thames, close to the National Theatre, with the dome of St Paul's Cathedral dominating the skyline. It was a wonderful location, right in the heart of London. In appointing me, my new employers made it clear that they wanted me to develop a major research project of my choice, and gave me a firm commitment that I would have the time to undertake this. They wanted the project to be theological, but also to engage with wider cultural issues. So what, I wondered, should I do?

It dawned on me that I could undertake a project that had, in many ways, been my heart's desire – to write a new biography of C.S. Lewis. The fiftieth anniversary of Lewis' death would be marked in November 2013. That would allow me four solid years to research and write the work, and a year to steer it through the publishing process. It was clear that a new biography was needed, given the obvious difficulties with existing ones, which did not seem to know what to make of Lewis' Irish roots, and generally offered a somewhat muddled account of his role at Oxford University. I had dual nationality, being both British and Irish, and I knew Oxford better than most.

Publishers were quickly arranged, and I mapped out what needed to be done. I would have to read everything that Lewis had written in chronological order, to get a sense of the development of his thought, and the shifts in his writing style. I would need to ransack archives in Oxford and Cambridge, to see if any documents had been overlooked by previous biographers, or if new resources had been uncovered. And so I happily set to work on what was to prove the most intellectually interesting and rewarding writing project of my life. My research turned up material that nobody had ever seen before, such as a letter from Lewis proposing J.R.R. Tolkien for the Nobel Prize in Literature, and the records of the Officer Cadet Battalion that had trained Lewis for combat in the First World War. My close reading of Lewis' writings led me to the unexpected conclusion that his discovery of God seemed to date from Trinity Term 1930, rather than endorsing Lewis' own memory of this event as having taken place in Trinity Term 1929. It was a small piece of scholarly detail, not of great importance to understanding Lewis' significance.

Yet one aspect of Lewis' life stood out as being particularly noteworthy for me, partly because I could relate easily and naturally to his concerns. Lewis was anxious that his conversion to Christianity would require him, as a matter of intellectual integrity, to set to one side one of the great loves of his life – Nordic mythology. He could not see how he could fit this old love into his new way of seeing the world, resulting from his religious conversion. Would he have to leave the Nordic myths behind, thus turning his back on something he cherished? If Christianity were *true*, then surely these myths were *false*? Or was there some way of accommodating both within his new faith, at present unknown to him?[1]

In the end, Lewis' concerns were resolved in a long conversation of September 1931 with his colleague Tolkien, allowing Lewis to see, for the first time, that Christianity told 'a story of a larger kind', and that this story created space for anticipations of its themes in the mythology of ancient Greece and the Nordic world. Shortly afterwards, Lewis wrote to his close friend Arthur Greeves, overwhelmed with excitement. Christianity brought the Nordic myths to fulfilment, he declared, disclosing the full reality that they captured only in part. He could not only retain his affection for them; he could use them in his elaboration of his Christian vision. The wooden and stale dichotomy of 'true' and 'false' was simply inadequate to describe the range of options at his disposal.

I experienced a concern just like this on my own conversion to Christianity, although while its intensity was comparable to that of Lewis, its focus was different. As this narrative makes clear, science was my supreme love as a young man, being both the heart of my professional aspirations and the catalyst for the life of my mind. Yet the 'official doctrine' – to borrow an apt phrase from Gilbert Ryle's classic *Concept of Mind* (1949) – was that religion and science were incompatible; indeed, that they were at war with each other. By embracing Christianity, I was anxious that I had taken a step that might separate, if not divorce, me from a field of study that I loved and had become an integral part of my life. So what was I to make of this 'official doctrine', endlessly repeated in the media?

My main reason for ignoring the trenchant affirmation of the incompatibility of science and religion was the obvious empirical fact that many intelligent scientists at Oxford at every level, from undergraduates to senior academics, held religious beliefs, and saw these as compatible with their science. I had no doubt that some noisy and influential individuals insisted that it was intellectually inconceivable to be a scientist and maintain religious beliefs; however, there was clearly a serious tension between this assertion and what was observable in the real world. After all, Albert Einstein – perhaps the most iconic natural scientist of the twentieth century – argued that meaningful human existence demanded the embracing of scientific, ethical, political and religious ideas, despite the fact that these ideas or values were generated using quite different research methods.[2]

Most scientists profess significant ethical and political views. Einstein, for example, was a socialist. Yet Einstein was adamant that he did not – and could not – derive his ethical or political views from the scientific method: 'Science can only ascertain what *is*, not what *should be*, and outside of its domain value judgements of all kinds remain necessary.'[3] Like the philosopher David Hume, Einstein was clear that there was no viable logical way of converting observations about the way the world functions to an understanding of how humans should behave.

Even so, Einstein believed that scientists *ought* to have moral and political views, even though those views would not be – and could not be – derived from the application of the scientific method. When the scientific method is understood properly, matters of ethics and politics are seen to lie beyond its scope.

The scientific method can teach us nothing beyond how facts are related to, and conditioned by, each other . . . The knowledge of what *is* does not open the door directly to what *should be*. One can have the clearest and most complete knowledge of what *is*, and yet not be able to

deduce from that what should be the *goal* of our human
aspirations.[4]

Ethics and politics are forms of human reflection that are
not scientific in their origin, but which are nevertheless
important aspects of the lives of all human beings – including scientists. Einstein also took the same position about
religion. Though defining 'religion' in a slightly idiosyn-
cratic manner, he insisted upon its cultural and intellectual
viability, and regarded it as integral to a meaningful human
existence.[5] Einstein set this position out in one of his best-
known aphorisms: 'science without religion is lame, religion
without science is blind'.[6]

So is science incompatible with ethics? Or politics? I
know of no scientist who would advocate such a position,
and there is no credible intellectual reason for drawing
such a ridiculous conclusion. It is the outcome of a patho-
logical form of intellectual tunnel vision unable or
unwilling to comprehend anything that lies beyond the
reach of empirical investigation. It does not follow that,
because science uses methods that differ from those of
ethics or theology, scientists therefore cannot hold ethical
or religious views. This bizarre conclusion would *only* be
valid if (a) all intellectual disciplines must adopt the same
research methods; and (b) the only valid research method
is that of the natural sciences. Neither (a) nor (b) stands up
to critical investigation.

Earlier in this narrative, I noted a turning point in my reflection about the relation of science and faith, brought about by
listening to a sermon by Charles A. Coulson preached in
Wadham College chapel and subsequently discussing its themes
with him. Coulson, who was Oxford's first Professor of

Theoretical Chemistry, held that science and Christian faith were to be seen as distinct yet complementary perspectives on a single, complex reality. Any full description of some complex reality requires its multiple perspectives to be identified, and then integrated into a larger overall account.

The point is easily applied to the multiple application of human reason to a range of intellectual territories, including the natural sciences, ethics, politics and religion. These may result from different methods of reasoning; that does not mean they are inconsistent, still less that they are incompatible. They represent the outcomes of rational reflection on distinct issues, which we weave together into our own individualised yet integrated way of understanding and acting within our world. Indeed, many would argue that a failure to connect and correlate these multiple aspects of our existence has led to an impoverished vision of life. The sociobiologist E.O. Wilson reintroduced the term 'consilience' to refer to his vision of interweaving insights from different fields of human knowledge to create a deepened understanding of the problems and possibilities that we face. 'We are drowning in information, while starving for wisdom.'[7]

So what of the pervasive cultural meme of the perennial and essential warfare between science and religion, exemplified by Bertrand Russell's anecdote of Calvin ridiculing Copernicus, which so influenced me while I was in the sixth form at Methody? I quickly grew suspicious of this ambitious universal principle, and wondered what professional historians made of it. It soon became clear that the idea of some perpetual 'warfare' of science and religious faith was a recent invention. For a start, scholars had challenged Russell's confident statement about Calvin ridiculing

Copernicus, and exposed his Calvin 'quote' as an invention – not necessarily on Russell's part, but probably in an unacknowledged source on which he had drawn.[8] Most of the popular myths about the 'warfare' of science and religion were invented in the late nineteenth century, and have now been systematically dismantled by historians, even though they are often repeated uncritically by the media and populist atheist apologists.

When I began to study quantum theory at Oxford, I began to realise that many of the writers in the field held carefully reasoned views on the relation of science and religious faith. I have already noted Albert Einstein's emphatic insistence on the need to hold science and religion together. Max Planck, widely regarded as the founder of quantum theory, argued that 'science and religion do not exclude each other, as many today believe or fear, but rather amplify and qualify each other'.[9] This is my settled view. Despite my earlier commitment to the notion of the 'warfare' of science and religious faith, I would now argue that Christianity and the natural sciences can – and should – engage in a constructive yet critical dialogical relationship. This dialogue is critical in its nature, even if it might be constructive in its outcomes.

The famous metaphor of the 'Two Books of God' dating back to the Renaissance, offers a helpful framework for such a critical dialogue, affirming the distinct identities of science and religion while holding that they can engage in dialogue on the basis of the essentially Christian assumption that both are rooted in the mind of God.[10] The metaphor was widely used by Renaissance writers to affirm and preserve the distinct character of both the natural sciences and Christian theology on the one hand, while acknowledging their capacity for constructive interaction on the other. The 'Two Books', it was argued, were both authored by God; might not God be known, then, in different ways and to different extents, through each of these books individually, and even more clearly through setting them side by side?

Christianity and the natural sciences are methodologically and conceptually distinct approaches to understanding and inhabiting our strange and complex world. Yet while these differences must be respected and safeguarded, there are potentially important and productive areas of discussion and reflection, allowing for the potential enrichment of each. We need such a dialogue, if we are to engage what the American philosopher John Dewey declared to be the 'deepest problem of modern life' – that we seem to have failed to manage to integrate our 'thoughts about the world' with our thoughts about 'value and purpose'.[11]

So I come back to Mary Midgley's idea of 'multiple maps' of reality, which has real potential to illuminate the relation of science and religious faith. Science is very good at taking the world apart so we can understand how it *works*. However, religious faith aims to put things back together so that we can see what they *mean*. A scientific map thus might be mainly concerned with functionality, whereas a religious map might focus on issues of value and meaning. Yet the maps can be laid over each other, enabling a new depth of overall perception, complementing each other.

I fully accept that not everyone will agree that my views about Christianity and the natural sciences are right, although they can certainly be justified. But what is perhaps most important is for each of us to develop our own personal synthesis, in which we bring together the evidence and concerns as we see them, and navigate our way to a workable and satisfying integration. Having tried to describe both the process by which I reached such a synthesis and its outcomes, I gladly leave it to my readers to judge their merits and develop their own.

21

The Irrationality of Faith?
The Doctrine of the Trinity

I was baptised in February 1953 in Down Cathedral, Downpatrick – or, to use its full name, the Cathedral Church of the Holy and Undivided Trinity. The Cathedral was built beside the grave of Patrick, the patron saint of Ireland, who used the shamrock as a teaching aid for the doctrine of the Trinity. As an atheist teenager, it seemed to me that I had been tainted from birth by an irrational belief system, which any fool could see was riddled with contradictions and inconsistencies. How could God be one and three? Surely this was illogical, a piece of nonsensical celestial mathematics? To parody Dante's *Divine Comedy*, it was as if the Cathedral's doors bore the motto 'abandon reason you who enter here'.

I was entirely open to being persuaded that there was a good reason, at present unknown to me, for taking this idea of the Trinity seriously; yet my attempts to find those reasons were utterly unsuccessful. None of the clergy whom I asked to explain this back in Ireland seemed to have given much thought to the question, and suggested that it was one of those mysteries it was probably best not to think about too much. Not unreasonably, I added this conspicuously irrational belief to the list of reasons why no thinking person could take Christianity seriously. As far as I was concerned, the Christian Creeds were a memorial to a world of dead ideas and a dying Church, lacking any capacity to connect with the modern world.

I no longer take this view, mainly for two reasons: a growing realisation of the difficulties that human beings encounter in grasping and representing *any* complex reality; and a deepened understanding of why this doctrine emerged, and what it achieves.

I specialised in the study of quantum theory at Oxford in the academic year 1971–2, welcoming the opportunity to examine leading writers in this field, including Albert Einstein, Werner Heisenberg and Max Planck. It was through reading them closely that I came to appreciate that the complexity of our universe vastly exceeds our ability to understand and represent it. Einstein, for example, held that nature was a magnificent structure that we can only grasp imperfectly, and could never hope to describe completely.

Heisenberg took a similar view, and set out the issues particularly well in an essay of 1941, declaring that scientific thinking 'always hovers over a bottomless depth', given the limits placed on human understanding.[1] Faced with the 'impenetrable darkness' of the universe, we struggle to find a language adequate to make sense of this 'mystery', rather than trying to reduce reality to what we can cope with. We see our universe darkly, being unable to break through its 'impenetrable darkness' and achieve the clarity of vision that is possible in matters of logic.

Heisenberg and other quantum theorists, such as Max Planck, had no difficulty in using the word 'mystery' to designate the complexity of the universe. However, this did not lead them to conclude that a mystery was basically an irrationality but something that exceeds human reason's capacity to investigate and describe fully. A complex reality requires multiple approaches and levels of description. Heisenberg insisted that we do not observe nature itself, but nature 'as it is disclosed by our methods of investigation'.[2] There is only one nature; yet to preserve it and to appreciate its depth and complexity, we have to use multiple research methods. Otherwise, we will end up equating nature with what one single perspective discloses – and in doing so, reduce and distort it. Our set of conceptual toolboxes – to use Mary Midgley's well-chosen phrase – gives us multiple perspectives on a complex reality, inviting us to integrate them into a single coherent account, while respecting and preserving the distinctiveness of each perspective.

Now these reflections on the immensity and complexity of the universe, and the limited capacity of the human mind to comprehend such a vast reality, have nothing *directly* to do with the doctrine of the Trinity. Yet when I began to study theology seriously five years later, I could see obvious connections between the two. The central problem is the natural human tendency to simplify complexities, distorting them in doing so. I began to think of the Trinity as the Christian attempt to put into words, however faltering and inadequate those might be, the totality of the rich and multi-faceted New Testament vision of God.

Andrew Louth, my Oxford tutor in early Christian theology (sometimes known as 'patristics') during 1977, helped me to see that the theologians of this formative age refused to dilute, simplify or reduce the core elements of the New Testament vision of God. Instead of assimilating their view of God to contemporary philosophical or cultural norms, they developed an intellectual framework and a distinct vocabulary which enfolded, correlated and safeguarded the core elements of this rich and distinctive vision of God, insisting on its fundamental unity while at the same time acknowledging its complexity.[3]

Early Christian writers such as Irenaeus of Lyons noted that the New Testament had three main interconnected understandings of God: God as the source of the universe; God as present and active in the person of Jesus of Nazareth in a focused and concentrated manner, reflected in Christ's capacity to disclose God and reconcile us to God; and God as present and active in the believer and the world through the Spirit. Irenaeus insisted that these three elements needed to be held together as integral elements of the New Testament's vision of God, and were not to be reduced or simplified for expedient purposes (in order to facilitate engagement with the various forms of monotheism found in secular Greek culture at that time for example).

I began to see connections between Irenaeus' approach to theology and a central theme in Aristotle's approach to science. For Aristotle, one of the core tasks of science was to 'save the phenomena' – in other words, to make sure that the process of scientific theorising respected and preserved the observations on which they were based, as it moved from observing the external world beyond us to constructing mental worlds within us. Like Aristotle, Irenaeus was concerned to identify and respect the 'phenomena' he found in the New Testament, and then to develop a conceptual framework for accommodating these coherently. The doctrine of the Trinity aims to distinguish between a *Christian* notion of God and *other* ideas of God, by weaving together all that Christians believe about God in a single whole, while affirming, valuing and naming each of its individual elements.

The vocabulary that early Christianity developed to express its rich vision of God causes difficulty today, in that the Latin term *persona*, which in Late Classical Antiquity had the meaning of a 'role played' (as, for example, in a drama), has now come to mean 'an individual being'. This could easily be misunderstood to imply that God consists of three distinct, individual beings, which is most emphatically not what the doctrine of the Trinity affirms or presupposes. It is not difficult to see how it could lead to the popular misunderstanding of 'one god yet three gods'. The Christian narrative is that of creation, redemption and transformation; yet each of these three distinct roles in the drama of salvation is played by one and the same God.[4]

The following term in 1977, I began the detailed study of systematic theology with Paul Fiddes, a rising young star of Oxford's Faculty of Theology, who had a particular interest in German-language theologians, especially the Swiss writer Karl Barth. Fiddes' enthusiasm for such theologians – including Wolfhart Pannenberg and Jürgen Moltmann – was infectious, and I continue to be firmly embedded within this theological world through his influence. Fiddes recommended that I read Barth's discussion of the doctrine of the Trinity while researching my essay on this topic. I found Barth engaging but bewildering, in that he seemed to think that the doctrine of the Trinity was to be regarded as some kind of revealed truth, which could serve as the basis for his theological system. Yet my reading of early Christian theology made it clear that this doctrine had *emerged* during the first four centuries as a means of integrating and correlating revealed truths. It was not a 'given'. Unpersuaded by Barth, I wondered if there were alternative ways of thinking about this doctrine that might be more convincing.

Happily, Fiddes had also recommended that I read

another Swiss theologian, Emil Brunner, on this topic. Brunner argued that the doctrine of the Trinity was not explicitly stated in the Christian Bible, but was 'the result of theological reflection upon the problem that is necessarily raised by the Christian *kerygma*'.[5] In other words, the Trinity was not a doctrine that was itself disclosed in the Bible, but rather the outcome of sustained engagement with the basic themes of the Christian proclamation, harmonising them into a coherent whole. I found this approach much more helpful, as it recognised that the Trinity was not itself a revealed doctrine but a concept that arose from reflection on revelation. The doctrine of the Trinity weaves together the core threads of the Christian vision of God, in order to ensure that God is never understood or proclaimed in an impoverished, truncated or distorted way. For Brunner, the concept of the Trinity was a 'theological safety doctrine' intended to protect 'the core faith of the Bible and of the church'. It interconnects the essential elements of a Christian doctrine of God, while leaving the question of the precise manner of their interaction open for further discussion.

This was the pattern I had seen while studying with Andrew Louth the previous term. Early Christian writers gradually developed the concept of the Trinity to enfold and safeguard the core elements of the New Testament's vision of God. If Brunner was right, the concept of the Trinity was a means of preserving the primal New Testament vision of God, at least holding its core elements together, and possibly illuminating and discerning their mutual relationship. I began to form a respect for Brunner, and hoped I might find a way of studying him in more detail later.[6]

So how do I now feel about the doctrine of the Trinity? I

no longer regard it as a rational embarrassment, but a powerful affirmation of the inability of human reason to take in the full richness of the reality of God, and the need to construct coherent mental frameworks which can encompass this single yet complex reality, avoiding the fragmentation and reductionist distortion that are the inevitable outcome of the uncritical application of 'reason' to 'reality'. It safeguards the core Christian vision of God, allowing it to be grasped yet not mastered. This Trinitarian vision in the end leads to worship and adoration, rather than mere rational comprehension.

Nevertheless I can now also see that any but the most superficial engagement with our world will end up facing the same issue that led to the formulation of the notion of the Trinity: the obstinate refusal of our cosmos to be mastered by human reason. As Werner Heisenberg pointed out, the deeper we penetrate into the mysteries of nature, the more we realise the inadequacy of existing concepts and vocabularies to do justice to what we encounter. And rather than distort nature by forcing it into existing frameworks of understanding and terminology, intellectual integrity requires us to develop new ones that are responsive to the realities we encounter. The doctrine of the Trinity does not impose paradoxes upon an uncomplicated reality found in the New Testament; the paradoxes are there already.

So, looking back on my past, how do I regard my earlier and somewhat premature dismissal of the idea of the Trinity? Naturally, I feel a certain degree of embarrassment at my belief that, as a sixteen-year-old, I had mastered the great questions of life. Yet my instincts at that time were sound. As the doctrine of the Trinity had been presented to me, it made no sense. Nobody explained to me what it really meant – perhaps because nobody thought it was worth explaining to an intellectually restless teenager. It was easy to see why I dismissed it as an irrationality, to be compared to the mathematical nonsense that $1 + 1 + 1 = 1$. It is equally clear why I later came to realise this was a total misunderstanding on my part, no matter how reasonable my conclusion may have been at the time. I had to learn to avoid reducing reality to what my mind could cope with, and instead to expand my mind to take in the vastness of reality.

And what of St Patrick? The poem *Lorica*, traditionally attributed to Patrick, surveys the landscape of theological and spiritual truths that are safeguarded and supported by the doctrine of the Trinity, like a hedge enfolding and protecting the lush pasturelands of County Down. Like Irenaeus before him, Patrick identified the 'phenomena' – the core themes of Christian belief in God – that need to be affirmed, and offered a Trinitarian conceptual framework to affirm and envelop them. The Trinity is the 'strong name' that holds together these insights about God's presence and activity in creating, redeeming and sustaining, respecting their individual significance, while at the same time plaiting these threads into a greater vision of God. If Patrick is right, the language of Christianity hovers over the brink of silence and song – silence, because it is inadequate to do justice to the vastness of its subject; and song, because it enables us to see, however dimly, that this 'vastness' has created space for us, inviting us to rejoice in being part of God's greater story.

I went back to Down Cathedral in August 2017, and stood for a few moments by Patrick's grave. It was a moment of reconnection with my past – but also a moment to acknowledge my reappraisal of this core theme of Christian faith. Thanks to those who taught me at Oxford, I had finally grasped something of what Patrick had seen in this doctrine that he made his own.

22

Through a Glass Darkly: Journeying through Doubt

The 1960s now seem a distant dream, a fading moment in cultural history tinged with a pervasive optimism and idealism, given intellectual resilience at the time by a belief that life's great questions could be sorted out definitively and unambiguously by the straight-talking no-nonsense Logical Positivism of A.J. Ayer, or the totalisations of Marxist ideology. I thought I was standing on the brink of a new age of clarity and certainty; in fact, it was simply an age of briefly fashionable new dogmas that were just as ephemeral as those they displaced.

I longed for a simple truth back then, resisting any recognition of complexity. I was seeking an objective, universal account of our world, independent of place and time, believing that the natural sciences and human reason, individually or collaboratively, were capable of delivering this secure and compelling rational truth. Indeed, for a while I believed I had found it, before gradually coming to realise, in a heartbreaking process of disillusionment, not merely that I had failed to find this rational Nirvana, but that it was not there to be found in the first place.

I have already reflected extensively upon the natural sciences. So what about philosophy, which some suggest offers complete and reliable answers to life's great questions? Despite welcome moments of rational transparency, our world seems frustratingly resistant to total intellectual mastery. While philosophy offers us a most impressive and engaging array of intellectual possibilities, there is no persuasive evidence that it has decisively resolved any of life's great questions. We can certainly take and defend committed positions on these questions, but these are to be seen as opinions and judgements, not secure knowledge.

In the early 2000s, I came to know the Polish philosopher and intellectual historian Leszek Kołakowski, whom Isaiah Berlin had helped to settle in Oxford after he was thrown out of his native Poland for publicly dissenting from Marxist orthodoxy. I had read his massive *Main Currents of Marxism*,[1] and enjoyed discussing its key themes with him, which confirmed my own suspicions about Marxism's intellectual overreach on the one hand, and its continuing utility as a tool of social analysis on the other. Impressed by the quality of his intellectual vision, I organised an international symposium on his work at All Souls College, Oxford, in October 2007. Yet what I found particularly significant was Kołakowski's critical views on the outcome of the philosophical enterprise in general, not simply its Marxist forms: 'Of the questions which have sustained European philosophy for two and a half millennia, not a single one has been answered to general satisfaction.'[2]

It is certainly true that some moral, philosophical and social beliefs achieve cultural dominance in certain cultural locations. Yet this is a social process, open to Marxist analysis. Although Kołakowski was critical of the Italian Marxist theoretician Antonio Gramsci, I found Gramsci particularly helpful in exploring how certain ideas – and not others of arguably equal or even greater intellectual plausibility – came to gain cultural acceptance, and occasionally outright dominance. As Gramsci pointed out, this cultural hegemony often arises through the deliberate manipulation of social processes in the service of vested interests, rather than because of the intrinsic excellence of those ideas.

It is thus no defence of the intellectual merits of a belief to point out that it has achieved widespread acceptance, perhaps even cultural dominance, or that it seems 'self-evident'. Such appearances of certainty may well be social constructions, not the outcome of critical intellectual analysis. The suggestion that we match the objective reliability of a belief with our subjective perception of its 'evidentness' fails to appreciate that this vague and undefined feeling of 'evidentness' is partly socially constructed, and collapses when subjected to critical interrogation.

The cultural history of philosophy discloses how human reasoning has been shaped by its historical and cultural contexts, suggesting that its solutions might be transient and local, rather than permanent and universal. Until recently, European philosophy has been strongly ethnocentric and monopolistic, treating Chinese and Indian philosophies with a haughty condescension. Breaking with the universal ambition of the bygone Western 'Age of Reason', it is now widely conceded that we need to speak of 'comparative philosophy', acknowledging how philosophical methods and assumptions (including those of the Enlightenment) are shaped by their cultural and historical contexts.

Happily, many philosophers are now alert to these changing perceptions of the relationship between philosophy and its shifting and unsettled cultural contexts. Mary Midgley, one of the most interesting of this group of historically and culturally enlightened philosophers, clearly appreciated the strengths and limits of the philosophical enterprise in the light of such a cultural and historical attentiveness. We philosophise in the midst of a changing world, and our philosophies can never be considered definitive or final.

> Philosophizing, in fact, is not a matter of solving one fixed set of puzzles. Instead, it involves finding the many particular ways of thinking that will be the most helpful as we try to explore this constantly changing world. Because the world – including human life – does constantly change, philosophical thoughts are never final. Their aim is always to help us through the present difficulty.[3]

Given the vulnerability of our faltering and fragile answers to life's ultimate questions, how do we cope with this uncertainty? After all, we are not logical calculating machines, but creatures who have realised the importance of intuition and emotions in helping us make decisions about our identities, aspirations and true meaning. The mechanical rational algorithms of the Enlightenment – so brilliantly parodied in Douglas Adams' *Hitchhiker's Guide to the Galaxy* (1979) – can only offer inadequate (and often incomprehensible) logical or mathematical answers to what are fundamentally *existential* questions, yet are so often posed as if they were *logical* or *scientific* questions.

Religious faith, seen by dogmatic rationalists as a violation of human reason, is better seen as illustrating the rational dilemma we *all* face in trying to make sense of things. Faith is a rejection of the rationalist delusion that we can have clear and secure knowledge of the answers to ultimate questions about our meaning, value and purpose. Perhaps it was once possible to believe that these grand questions could be definitively answered by an appeal to compelling or overwhelming evidence; yet the discussion has moved on, and we must leave such illusions behind us. We can give answers that we believe to be warranted and justified, but we cannot prove they are right and reliable, even though we believe that they are so. Faith is a willingness, even a determination, to cope with this half-lit world, believing with our minds and trusting in our hearts that we can find good answers to our questions, while tantalisingly knowing we cannot prove them to be true.

There is indeed a single human faculty of reason; yet this gives rise to multiple rationalities.[4] There are many ways in which human beings can be rational, one of which is the monopolistic approach associated with the 'Age of Reason'; another is the distinct rationality of the Christian faith. Early Christian writers constantly reaffirmed that their faith was *logikos* – rational, in the sense of corresponding to a deep understanding of fundamental truths about our situation within a greater order of things. But these deep truths are better understood as *wisdom*, rather than *knowledge*, in that they enable us to live meaningfully in a complex world, coping with human suffering, vulnerability, trauma and failure.

Wisdom, however, is not a set of abstract ideas, but something that is best grasped through exemplars – living human beings who are seen to embody these ideas, and are able to express them in practice. We learn what it means to be good, faithful and caring through encounters with people who compellingly exemplify these qualities and evoke both admiration on our part and a desire to emulate them. Christianity speaks of the embodiment of wisdom and goodness in Jesus Christ, using the language of 'incarnation' to express the core belief that Christ manifests and embodies divine wisdom, while nevertheless enduring rejection, suffering and crucifixion. Christ exemplifies, embodies and enables the Christian capacity to cope with meaninglessness, incoherence, uncertainty and tragedy. Part of Christian discipleship is the development of the 'mind of Christ' (1 Corinthians 2.16), a habit of thought and reasoning that allows us to cultivate resilience in the face of life's enigmas and traumas.

Christianity does not merely offer a new way of beholding our world, but an enhanced capacity to live within that world and cope with its uncertainty and complexity, as well as our own frailty and failings. It enables us to confront glib and shallow accounts of our situation, such as the superficial rationalism of the Enlightenment or the facile optimism of an ideology of 'positive thinking', which seeks to exorcise any recognition of the darker and more disturbing aspects of human nature or creation. Reality is complex and ambivalent; wisdom demands that we recognise this, rather than crudely forcing it to be uniformly simple and positive. Intellectual violence is unable to suppress this darker truth about our world, which Christianity has affirmed and confronted, rather than implausibly denied.

Wisdom is a form of knowledge that eschews simple and superficial readings of reality, driven by an intolerance of uncertainty. It demands a deep immersion in the paradoxes and problems of living in a world that is resistant to quick and easy interpretations. The 'wise' are those who are willing to adapt their patterns of thought and life to this complex world, rather than attempting to force the world to conform to their preconceived ideas. Wisdom demands that we respect and actively embrace a deep mystery, something that transcends the boundaries of human comprehension.

G.K. Chesterton declared that, by acknowledging one thing to be mysterious, everything else becomes lucid. As Newton found in setting out the idea of gravity, and Christians in expressing the notion of the Trinity, we often find that something that we do not – and perhaps cannot – fully understand allows us to understand everything else. Paradoxically, mysteries have a remarkable capacity to illuminate.

We do indeed see through a glass darkly (1 Corinthians 13.12), being captives to our limited capacity to behold and understand, and the fragility of the truths on which we base our lives. That's why we attach ourselves to others for company and solidarity, holding on to a vision of reality and embodiment of wisdom, which in turn holds us, encouraging us to probe and discover its depths and riches. Somehow, the shadows of the cosmos seem softer and more bearable when we journey in company – and in *hope*, knowing that someone has walked through that darkness before us, blazing a trail we can follow.

23

A Loose Ending

Earlier, I mentioned how I had been invited to compose an imagined letter to myself as a teenager. But suppose I had written a letter to my future self when I was sixteen, securely sealed in an envelope marked 'Do not open until you are 66'? What, I often wonder, might that have said? Would I have had any idea of the form my journey would actually take? I doubt it. While I could not have predicted this story, nor can I tell you how it will end, I can at least look back on it, and reflect on its unpredictable turns.

Some say that our best hope of making sense of our lives is to write them down. This short book has told my story of discovering and exploring a strange new world, a mysterious island on which I found myself unexpectedly shipwrecked. It explains how I learned to cope with uncertainty, without falling into a radical scepticism ('since everything is uncertain, you can't believe anything') or thoroughgoing relativism ('since everything is uncertain, it doesn't matter what you believe'). There are no heroes or villains. It is neither typical nor normative. I have no scores to settle or virtues to signal. It's just my own account of my attempts to make sense of life, and work out who I really am and what I was meant to be doing. And perhaps more importantly, it's about the travelling companions I came to know and respect along the way, who helped me grow and develop.

Perhaps the most important thing I have learned is that our convictions arise from our personal histories – from our interactions with others, both living and dead. In setting out in this book *what* I now think, I cannot help but tell the story of *how* I came to think in this way, and *who* helped me to do so. My ideas and my history intersect and overlap. It will be obvious from this narrative how much I owe to others in developing my ideas.

The journey of exploration and discovery that I have described in this short work is thus not that of a solitary individual, detached from others; it is about both being *helped to think* and being *accompanied* by others who travel on the road of faith. This brief narrative of my own journeys of exploration will make it clear how much I am indebted to others, living and dead. I owe so much to so many that I cannot even begin to name them all, even if some – such as C.S. Lewis – stand out in my memory, and are referenced extensively in my writings. They helped me expand my vision of reality, rather than being limited to my own personal perspective, by challenging me to consider whether I might have missed something that they have seen, and reassuring me that I was not alone in facing up to problems and seeking wisdom.

Whatever the future holds, I hope I will continue to journey with travelling companions who will help me cope with that new world, living with uncertainty while journeying in hope. Yet I have a small ambition for that future. One day, I shall buy myself a good astronomical telescope, and look again at the rich star-fields of the Milky Way and the fuzzy galaxies beyond our own as I once did in the 1960s, and have never done since. Perhaps looking again at these faint patches of light in the enveloping darkness might help me recapture something of that sense of wonder that I knew back then, which motivated my love for science and ended up leading me to see myself and the universe in a new and unexpected way.

Some Notes on My Books

The narrative of discovery and exploration presented in this book will raise many questions, not least about the nature of Christianity, the relation of science and faith, and the limits of human knowledge. These are touched on at many points in my writings. This final section notes some of my writings that my correspondence suggests readers find particularly accessible or interesting, listed by topic. You will find much more information about my books and other publications, as well as free video and audio presentations, on my website: alistermcgrath.net. Everything on this website can be downloaded free of charge and used as you please, provided it is not for commercial gain.

Theological Textbooks

Christian Theology: An Introduction, 6th edition (Chichester: Wiley, 2016).

Theology: The Basics, 4th edition (Chichester: Wiley, 2018).

The Christian Theology Reader, 5th edition (Chichester: Wiley, 2016).

Theology: The Basic Readings, 3rd edition (Chichester: Wiley, 2018).

Christianity

The Landscape of Faith (London: SPCK, 2016).
Christianity: An Introduction, 3rd edition (Chichester: Wiley, 2016).

The History of Christian Thought

Iustitia Dei: A History of the Christian Doctrine of Justification, 4th edition (Cambridge: Cambridge University Press, 2020).
Historical Theology: An Introduction to the History of Christian Thought, 2nd edition (Chichester: Wiley, 2012).

C.S. Lewis

C.S. Lewis – A Life: Eccentric Genius, Reluctant Prophet (London: Hodder & Stoughton, 2013).
Deep Magic, Dragons and Talking Mice: How Reading C.S. Lewis Can Change Your Life (London: Hodder & Stoughton, 2014).

The New Atheism

Dawkins' God: From the Selfish Gene to the God Delusion, 2nd edition (Oxford: Wiley-Blackwell, 2015).
The Dawkins Delusion? Atheist Fundamentalism and the Denial of the Divine (London: SPCK, 2007). This book was co-written with Joanna Collicutt.

Science and Faith

Inventing the Universe: Why We Can't Stop Talking About Science, Faith and God (London: Hodder & Stoughton, 2015).

Enriching Our Vision of Reality: Theology and the Natural Sciences in Dialogue (London: SPCK, 2016).

The Great Mystery: Science, God and the Human Quest for Meaning (London: Hodder & Stoughton, 2017).

A Theory of Everything (That Matters): A Short Guide to Einstein, Relativity and the Future of Faith (London: Hodder & Stoughton, 2019).

Science and Religion: An Introduction, 3rd edition (Chichester: Wiley, 2020).

Natural Theology

The Open Secret: A New Vision for Natural Theology (Oxford: Blackwell, 2008).

A Fine-Tuned Universe: The Quest for God in Science and Theology (Louisville, KY: Westminster John Knox Press, 2009).

Darwinism and the Divine: Evolutionary Thought and Natural Theology (Oxford: Wiley-Blackwell, 2011).

Re-Imagining Nature: The Promise of a Christian Natural Theology (Oxford: Wiley-Blackwell, 2016).

Articles

I have written more than 120 research articles. Three of these may be helpful in exploring the ideas explored in this work:

'Christianity', in Massimo Pigliucci, Skye Cleary and Daniel A. Kaufman (eds), *How to Live a Good Life* (New York: Vintage, 2019), pp. 166–82.

'Loving Science, Discovering God: An Autobiographical Reflection on Science and Theology', *Theology and Science*, vol. 17, no. 4 (2019), pp. 431–43.

'*Metanoia*: Jesus, Paul, and the Transformation of the Believing Mind', in Craig A. Evans and Aaron W. White (eds), *Who Created Christianity? Fresh Approaches to the Relationship Between Paul and Jesus* (Peabody, MA: Hendrickson, 2020).

Notes

1 A Curious Mind

1 'Leica' was simply a contracted form of 'Leitz Camera'. I was later able to identify the year of manufacture (1903) from the microscope's serial number, when the company's production records were made available online.

2 Science as Sense-Making

1 C.P. Snow, *The Search* (Harmondsworth: Penguin, 1965), p. 33. This novel is partly autobiographical; Snow himself studied for a University of London degree in physics in the 1920s.

2 Joseph Conrad, *Chance* (London: Methuen, 1914), p. 4.

3 A Sceptical Chemist

1 Betrand Russell, *A History of Western Philosophy* (London: George Allen & Unwin, 1950), p. 487.

4 Dreaming of Oxford

1 I later discovered that my hastily conceived hypothesis had been proposed in some research articles dealing with the Jahn–Teller effect that were published in 1969 and 1970.

5   A Crisis of Faith

1 Arthur Koestler, *The Ghost in the Machine* (London: Hutchinson, 1967), p. 78.

2 Arthur Koestler, *The Invisible Writing* (London: Collins, 1954), p. 19.

3 Arthur Koestler, *Darkness at Noon* (London: Jonathan Cape, 1940), p. 142.

4 Bertrand Russell, *A History of Western Philosophy* (London: George Allen & Unwin, 1950), p. 2.

6   Discovering God

1 For my extended treatment of Einstein, completing the process of reflection I began in 1971, see Alister McGrath, *A Theory of Everything (That Matters): A Short Guide to Einstein, Relativity and the Future of Faith* (London: Hodder & Stoughton, 2019).

7   Shipwrecked on an Island of Faith

1 *Macbeth*, Act 1, scene 7, line 27.

2 Henry Miller, *Big Sur and the Oranges of Hieronymus Bosch* (New York: New Directions, 1957), p. 25.

3 Eugene Wigner, 'The Unreasonable Effectiveness of Mathematics', *Communications on Pure and Applied Mathematics*, vol. 13 (1960), pp. 1–14.

8   A Travelling Companion: C.S. Lewis

1 C.S. Lewis, *They Asked for a Paper* (London: Geoffrey Bles, 1962), p. 165.

2 The final four of this suite of twelve essays were 'Is Theology Poetry?', 'Transposition', 'On Obstinacy in Belief' and the

sermon 'The Weight of Glory'. These are, in my view, Lewis' finest short works.

3 Lewis, *They Asked for a Paper*, pp. 187–8.

9   The First Mountain: Science

1 Technically, the probe used the 9-anthroyloxy fluorophore (the fluorescent region of the probe), attached to palmitic acid, which mimicked the structure of lipid bilayers.

2 The paper was published early the next year: A.E. McGrath, C.G. Morgan and G.K. Radda, 'Photobleaching: A Novel Fluorescence Method for Diffusion Studies in Lipid Systems', *Biochimica et Biophysica Acta*, vol. 426 (1976), pp. 173–85.

10   The Second Mountain: Theology

1 A.E. McGrath, C.G. Morgan and G.K. Radda, 'Positron Lifetimes in Phospholipid Dispersions', *Biochimica et Biophysica Acta*, vol. 466 (1977), pp. 367–72; idem, 'Lipid Asymmetry, Clustering and Molecular Motion in Biological Membranes and Their Models', in S. Abrahamsson and I. Pascher (eds), *Nobel Foundation Symposium: Biological Membranes and Their Models* (New York: Plenum Press, 1977), pp. 389–407.

11   Wandering: Searching for a Calling

1 In the end, I published this research as three books: *Luther's Theology of the Cross: Martin Luther's Theological Breakthrough* (1985); *Iustitia Dei: A History of the Christian Doctrine of Justification* (1986); and *The Intellectual Origins of the European Reformation* (1987). All three were updated in later editions.

2 C.S. Lewis, *Mere Christianity* (London: HarperCollins, 2002), pp. 11–12.

12   Oxford: Finding a Calling

1 For media comments on the sermon, see Victoria Combe, 'Church is Urged to Challenge Modish Opinions', *Daily Telegraph*, 15 November 2000.

2 Alister E. McGrath, *Dawkins' God: Genes, Memes, and the Meaning of Life* (Oxford: Blackwell Publishing, 2004). A second edition was published in 2015, incorporating assessment of Dawkins' later work *The God Delusion* (2006).

13   The Two Peaks: The View from the Top

1 Alister E. McGrath, *The Genesis of Doctrine* (Oxford: Blackwell Publishing, 1990). The Bampton Lectures are a series of eight lectures, delivered every other year on Sundays in the University Church of St Mary, and should not be confused with regular university theology lectures.

2 The best, in my view, is Rudolf Langthaler, *Warum Dawkins unrecht hat: Eine Streitschrift* (Freiburg: Verlag Karl Alber, 2015). Sadly, this has not yet been translated into English.

3 Fortunately, a few academics prove able to meet this challenge, such as my Oxford colleague Diarmaid MacCulloch. Regrettably, I found it rather more difficult.

14   On Reconsidering What Once Seemed Obvious

1 I joined seven others in drafting such letters: *Church Times*, 9 February 2018.

2 Alfred North Whitehead, *The Concept of Nature* (Cambridge: Cambridge University Press, 1920), p. 104.

3 Hermann Hesse, 'Die Sehnsucht unser Zeit nach einer Weltanschauung', *Uhu*, vol. 2 (1926), pp. 3–14. Hesse was here commenting on the core values of the ill-fated Weimar Republic, which seemed to him to lack any transcendent ground or possess any historical stability.

15   Seeing Reality: Christianity as a 'Big Picture'

1 William James, *Principles of Psychology* (Cambridge, MA: Harvard University Press, 1981), p. 462.

2 Alexander Wood, *In Pursuit of Truth: A Comparative Study in Science and Religion* (London: Student Christian Movement, 1927), p. 102.

3 Woolf uses her characters Clarissa Dalloway and Septimus Warren Smith in *Mrs Dalloway* to explore these experiences and their implications.

4 Dante, *Paradiso* XXXIII, lines 55–6: cf. John D. Sinclair, *Dante, The Divine Comedy*, vol. 3 (Oxford: Oxford University Press, 1961), p. 480.

5 Peter Medawar, 'Hypothesis and Imagination', *Times Literary Supplement*, 25 October 1963.

6 See Arnon Levy and Peter Godfrey-Smith (eds), *The Scientific Imagination* (Oxford: Oxford University Press, 2020).

7 William James, *The Will to Believe* (New York: Dover Publications, 1956), p. 51.

8 Think of Dante's core theme of *visibile parlare*, 'speaking visibly' in the *Purgatorio*, canto X, line 95.

9 C.S. Lewis, 'Imagery in the Last Eleven Cantos of Dante's "Comedy"', in *Studies in Medieval and Renaissance Literature* (Cambridge: Cambridge University Press, 1998), pp. 78–93; quote at p. 90. Note also Lewis' enigmatic comments about his own experience at this point.

10 Austin Farrer, 'The Christian Apologist', in Jocelyn Gibb (ed.), *Light on C.S. Lewis* (London: Geoffrey Bles, 1965), pp. 23–45; quote at p. 37.

11 Ludwig Wittgenstein, *Philosophical Investigations*, 3rd edition (Oxford: Blackwell, 1968), §115.

12 For a good discussion of this point, see Henk W. de Regt, 'Visualization as a Tool for Understanding', *Perspectives on Science*, vol. 22, no. 3 (2014), pp. 377–96.

13 George Herbert, *Works*, ed. F.E. Hutchinson (Oxford: Clarendon Press, 1941), p. 184.

14 Henry Miller, *On Writing* (New York: New Directions, 1964), p. 37.

15 C.S. Lewis, *They Asked for a Paper* (London: Geoffrey Bles, 1962), p. 165.

16   Revisiting Plato's Cave: On Darkness, Shadows and Light

1 Plato, *The Republic*, trans. H.D.P. Lee, 3rd edition (London: Penguin Books, 2007), pp. 89–90.

2 A good starting point is Dale Hall, 'Interpreting Plato's Cave as an Allegory of the Human Condition', *Apeiron: A Journal for Ancient Philosophy and Science*, vol. 14, no. 2 (1980), pp. 74–86.

3 Frances W. Weber, 'Unamuno's *Niebla*: From Novel to Dream', *Publications of the Modern Language Association*, vol. 88, no. 2 (1973), 209–18.

4 Lewis, *They Asked for a Paper* (London: Geoffrey Bles, 1962), p. 200.

5 John Banville, *The Sea* (New York: Vintage Books, 2005), p. 53.

17   Longing for Certainty: Proof, Faith and Doubt

1 Alasdair C. MacIntyre, *Whose Justice? Which Rationality?* (Notre Dame, IN: University of Notre Dame Press, 1988), p. 357.

2 I am not entirely sure that I managed to make a distinction between a subjective perception of certainty and an objectively grounded certainty – or, indeed, that I realised how these two aspects of the question so often became entangled.

3 For Dawkins' similar views on this issue, see Richard Dawkins, *The Selfish Gene,* 2nd edition (Oxford: Oxford University Press, 1989), p. 330.

4 For documentation and criticism of this widespread trend in the teaching of science in British schools, see Jonathan Osborne, 'Teaching Critical Thinking? New Directions in Science Education', *School Science Review*, vol. 95, no. 352 (2014), pp. 53–62; quote at p. 54.

5   Thomas Bonk, *Underdetermination: An Essay on Evidence and the Limits of Natural Knowledge* (Dordrecht: Springer, 2008).

6   These problems are generally agreed to remain unsolved: Colin Howson, *Hume's Problem: Induction and the Justification of Belief* (Oxford: Oxford University Press, 2000).

7   Charles Darwin, *Origin of Species*, 6th edition (London: John Murray, 1872), p. 444. Darwin does not mention Hume by name here, but delineates his position.

8   See especially Bertrand Russell, *Essays in Skepticism* (New York: Philosophical Library, 1963), pp. 83–4; *Bertrand Russell Speaks His Mind* (London: Barker, 1960), p. 20.

9   For the unease that Dawkins' populist views on science have caused within the scientific community, see David R. Johnson, Elaine Howard Ecklund, Di Di, and Kirstin R.W. Matthews, 'Responding to Richard: Celebrity and (Mis)Representation of Science', *Public Understanding of Science*, vol. 27, no. 5 (2018), pp. 535–49.

10 Jeanette Winterson, *Why Be Happy When You Could Be Normal?* (London: Vintage, 2012), p. 68.

11 Bas van Fraassen, *The Empirical Stance* (New Haven, CT: Yale University Press, 2002), pp. 47–8.

12 Richard Dawkins, *The Selfish Gene*, 2nd edition (Oxford: Oxford University Press, 1989), p. 330.

13 Milan Kundera, *The Unbearable Lightness of Being* (London: Faber & Faber, 1995), p. 135.

18   Delusion: Faith as Wish-Fulfilment?

1   Alister E. McGrath, *Iustitia Dei: A History of the Christian Doctrine of Justification*, 4th edition (Cambridge: Cambridge University Press, 2020).

2   Thomas Nagel, *The Last Word* (Oxford: Oxford University Press, 1997), p.130.

3   Aldous Huxley, *Ends and Means: An Inquiry into the Nature of Ideals* (New Brunswick, NJ: Transaction Publishers, 2012), p. 312.

4 Jonathan Haidt, *The Righteous Mind: Why Good People Are Divided by Politics and Religion* (New York: Pantheon Books, 2012).

5 Adrian Bardon, *The Truth About Denial: Bias and Self-Deception in Science, Politics, and Religion* (New York: Oxford University Press, 2019).

6 Isaiah Berlin, 'The Pursuit of the Ideal', in *The Crooked Timber of Humanity* (New York: Knopf, 1991), pp. 1–19; quote at p. 14.

7 John Gray, *Isaiah Berlin* (Princeton: Princeton University Press, 2006), pp. 74–110. The American philosopher Robert Pasnau developed a similar approach in his 2014 Isaiah Berlin lectures at Oxford, which I had the pleasure of attending. These lectures were later published as Robert Pasnau, *After Certainty: A History of Our Epistemic Ideals and Illusions* (Oxford: Oxford University Press, 2017), pp. 1–138.

19 Maps of Reality: Coping with the Complexity of Our World

1 Lewis' three lectures were published as *The Abolition of Man* (London: Oxford University Press, 1944).

2 These were published in an expanded form as Alister E. McGrath, *The Open Secret: A New Vision for Natural Theology* (Oxford: Blackwell, 2008).

3 I later discovered her full account of this issue in Mary Midgley, *Science and Poetry* (London: Routledge, 2001), pp. 170–213.

4 Werner Heisenberg, 'Die Kopenhagener Deutung der Quantentheorie', in *Physik und Philosophie* (Stuttgart: Hirzel, 2007), pp. 67–85; quote at p. 85.

5 John S. Habgood, *Theology and the Sciences* (London: The Athenaeum, 1998), p. 3. I explore Habgood's approach in Alister E. McGrath, 'An Undivided Mind: John Habgood on Science and Religion', *Journal of Anglican Studies* 19, no. 1 (2021): 68–83.

6 John Habgood, *Confessions of a Conservative Liberal* (London: SPCK, 1988), p. 95.

7 Peter Harrison, *The Territories of Science and Religion* (Chicago: University of Chicago Press, 2015).

20 Science and Faith: Conflicting or Enriching?

1 For a full account of this pivotal moment in Lewis' life, see Alister E. McGrath, *C.S. Lewis – A Life* (London: Hodder & Stoughton, 2013), pp. 147–51.

2 For a detailed analysis, see Alister McGrath, *A Theory of Everything (That Matters): A Short Guide to Einstein, Relativity and the Future of Faith* (London: Hodder & Stoughton, 2019).

3 Albert Einstein, *Out of My Later Years* (New York: Littlefield, Adams & Co., 1967), p. 29 (emphasis in original).

4 Albert Einstein, *Ideas and Opinions* (New York: Crown Publishers, 1954), pp. 41–2.

5 The best study remains Max Jammer, *Einstein and Religion: Physics and Theology* (Princeton, NJ: Princeton University Press, 1999).

6 Einstein, *Ideas and Opinions*, p. 46.

7 Edward O. Wilson, *Consilience: The Unity of Knowledge* (New York: Vintage, 1999), p. 294.

8 Edward Rosen, 'Calvin's Attitude Towards Copernicus', *Journal of the History of Ideas*, vol. 21 (1960), pp. 431–41.

9 Max Planck, *Religion und Naturwissenschaft* (Leipzig: J.A. Barth, 1938), p. 31: 'Religion und Naturwissenschaft – sie schließen sich nicht aus, wie manche heutzutage glauben oder fürchten, sondern sie ergänzen und bedingen einander'.

10 For its origin and development, see Kenneth J. Howell, *God's Two Books: Copernican Cosmology and Biblical Interpretation in Early Modern Science* (Notre Dame, IN: University of Notre Dame Press, 2002).

11 John Dewey, *The Quest for Certainty* (New York: Capricorn Books, 1960), p. 255.

21 The Irrationality of Faith? The Doctrine of the Trinity

1 Werner Heisenberg, *Die Ordnung der Wirklichkeit* (Munich: Piper Verlag, 1989), p. 44.

2 Werner Heisenberg, 'Die Kopenhagener Deutung der Quantentheorie', in *Physik und Philosophie* (Stuttgart: Hirzel, 2007), p. 85.

3 This theme is more fully developed in Louth's outstanding later work, *Discerning the Mystery: An Essay on the Nature of Theology* (Oxford: Clarendon Press, 1983). Reading this work on its appearance reminded me of how much I had learned from Louth's tutorials.

4 This is a gross simplification of a complex point. For much better discussions, see Kathryn Tanner, *Jesus, Humanity and the Trinity: A Brief Systematic Theology* (Minneapolis, MN: Fortress Press, 2001); Keith Ward, *Christianity: A Beginner's Guide* (Oxford: Oneworld, 2007), pp. 80–94. A useful discussion can also be found in Alister E. McGrath, *Christian Theology: An Introduction*, 6th edition (Chichester: Wiley, 2016), pp. 299–326.

5 Emil Brunner, *Dogmatics*, vol. 1 (Cambridge: Lutterworth, 1949), p. 236. The Greek word *kerygma* means 'proclamation'.

6 Happily, I did. While researching early sixteenth-century Swiss humanism in Zurich in the late 1980s, I found time to read and reflect on the University of Zurich's holdings of Brunner's works, and eventually published a monograph on his theology: Alister E. McGrath, *Emil Brunner: A Reappraisal* (Oxford: Wiley-Blackwell, 2016).

22 Through a Glass Darkly: Journeying through Doubt

1 Leszek Kołakowski, *Main Currents of Marxism: Its Rise, Growth, and Dissolution*, 3 vols (Oxford: Clarendon Press, 1978).

2   Leszek Kołakowski, *Metaphysical Horror* (Chicago: University of Chicago Press, 2001), pp. 1–2. This point is repeatedly made in recent reflections on the limits of philosophy: see, for example, John Shand, 'Philosophy Makes No Progress, So What Is The Point Of It?', *Metaphilosophy*, vol. 48 (2017), pp. 284–95.

3   Mary Midgley, *What Is Philosophy For?* (London: Bloomsbury Academic, 2018), p. 6. This is Midgley's final published work, and can be seen as a definitive statement of her mature views on the tasks and outcomes of philosophy. For my own assessment of Midgley, see Alister E. McGrath, 'The Owl of Minerva: Reflections on the Theological Significance of Mary Midgley.' Heythrop Journal 61, no. 5 (2020), pp. 852–64.

4   Karl-Otto Apel and Matthias Kettner (eds), *Die eine Vernunft und die vielen Rationalitäten* (Frankfurt am Main: Suhrkamp, 1996).

HODDER &
STOUGHTON

Hodder & Stoughton is the UK's
leading Christian publisher,
with a wide range of books from
the bestselling authors in the UK
and around the world ranging from
Christian lifestyle and theology to
apologetics, testimony and fiction.
We also publish the world's
most popular Bible translation
in modern English, the New
International Version, renowned
for its accuracy and readability.